ENGLISH
Direct
3

John Foster
Keith West

Collins Educational
An imprint of HarperCollinsPublishers

Published by Collins Educational

An imprint of HarperCollins*Publishers* Ltd
77–85 Fulham Palace Road
London W6 8JB

© HarperCollins*Publishers* Ltd 1998

First published 1998

10 9 8 7 6 5

www.**Collins**Education.com
On-line support for schools and colleges

ISBN 000 323 070 8

John Foster and Keith West assert the moral right to be identified as the authors of this work.

British Library Cataloguing in Publication Data.
A catalogue record for this book is available from the British Library.

Commissioned by Domenica de Rosa

Edited by Kim Richardson

Project management by Lisa English

Picture research by Katie Anderson

Production by Susan Cashin

Design and layout by Ken Vail Graphic Design, Cambridge

Cover design by Ken Vail Graphic Design, Cambridge

Cover photographs: Getty Images and Telegraph Colour Library

Printed and bound by Printing Express Ltd, Hong Kong

Acknowledgements

The following permissions to reproduce material are gratefully acknowledged. Numbers refer to pages.

Illustrations

John Walmsley (6, 11, 22, 34, 38, 70); Phil Smith (Sylvie Poggio Artists Agency) (7, 37, 74, 94, 95); Alastair Gray (Sylvie Poggio Artists Agency) (8, 27, 40, 51, 59); John Birdsall Photography (10, 32, 71); Telegraph Colour Library (13, 18, 21, 36, 39, 42); Angus Mill (14, 23, 24, 25, 50, 80); Sarah Warburton (Sylvie Poggio Artists Agency) (15, 17); Sarah Geeves (20, 28, 43, 53, 55, 68, 85); Penguin Books Ltd (26); Judy Brown (30, 31, 75, 79); RSPCA Photolibrary (35); Getty Images (45 top right, 78, 86, 87, 88 bottom); Famous (45 middle, 46); Melanie Mansfield (Sylvie Poggio Artists Agency) (49); BBC (60, 88 top, 89); Paul McCaffrey (Sylvie Poggio Artists Agency) (61-67); Wales News and Picture Service (72); Travel Ink (76 both); Public Relations Department, Borough of Basingstoke and Deane (84); Mike Lacey (Simon Girling & Associates) (92).

Text extracts

Extract from *Zlata's Diary* is by Zlata Filipovic, translated by Christina Pribichevich-Zoric, published by Viking 1994 (8); The five book reviews are from *Our Choice 2*, published by the Young Book Trust (24-25); The extracts on animal experimentation are from *What's The Big Idea? Animal Testing* by Anita Ganeri, published by Hodder Children's Books (38-39); 'The Ballad of Homeless Jack' and 'Write-a-Rap Rap' are both by Tony Mitton (42, 46); 'Health Care' by Benjamin Zephaniah is from *Funky Chickens*, published by Puffin (48); 'Before You Perform Your Rap...' is by Martin Glynn, from *Doin Me Ed In*, compiled by David Orme, published by Macmillan (48); 'Teenage Meanage' is by Yvonne Mitto, from *Doin Me Ed In*, compiled by David Orme, published by Macmillan (49); 'Steve Taylor' is an extract from *If This Is The Real World*, by Brian Keaney, published by Oxford University Press (51); 'Scrumping' is an extract from *That's How It Was*, by Maureen Duffy, published by Virago Press (52); 'Belfast Saturday' is an extract by Jenni Russell from *Children as Writers*, published by Heinemann Educational (53-55); 'Now then Sir, why are you driving this old croc?' is from *The Daily Mail*, 7 February 1998 (72); 'Paddle Power' is from *The Young Telegraph*, 2 August 1997 (76); The material in 'Somerwest World' is reproduced courtesy of Butlin's Ltd (81); The material in 'Disneyland Paris Resort Hotels' is reproduced courtesy of Disneyland® Paris and Leger Travel Ltd (82-83); Extract on Malta is from the 'Thomson Winter Sun' brochure, October 1996-April 1997, and is reproduced courtesy of Thomson Tour Operators (86); Extract on Malta is from the *Children's Britannica*, published by Encyclopædia Britannica International Ltd (87); Extract from *Starting Out* by Anthony Horowitz, published by Hodder and Stoughton (92-93).

Whilst every effort has been made to contact the copyright-holders, this has not proved possible in every case.

Contents

English Direct – Complete Coverage of the National Curriculum

English Direct 1 Year 7	English Direct 2 Year 8	English Direct 3 Year 9
Personal Writing *Topic* Autobiography *Language focus* Drafting	**Personal Writing** *Topics* A class who's who; My life; Letter to a penfriend *Language focus* Capital letters and full stops; Letter writing; Verbs and tenses	**Personal Writing 6** *Topic* Diaries *Language focus* Prefixes and suffixes
Conveying Information *Topics* Messages and instructions; School rules; Class outings *Language focus* Letter writing; IT skills	**Conveying Information** *Topics* My hobby; Animal fact files; An A–Z of sports *Language focus* Drafting and delivering a talk	**Conveying Information 14** *Topics* Factsheets; Leaflets *Language focus* Sentences and paragraphs; Letter writing
Expressing Opinions *Topics* TV programmes; Films and videos *Language focus* Sentences; Capital letters	**Expressing Opinions** *Topics* Pop shows; CDs; Book reviews *Language focus* Spelling	**Expressing Opinions 22** *Topics* Book reviews; A book project; Computer games *Language focus* Commas; Spelling
Developing Arguments *Topic* Letters to newspapers *Language focus* Drafting; Punctuation	**Developing Arguments** *Topics* Heroes and heroines; The school I'd like; Letters to newspapers *Language focus* Paragraphs; Conjunctions; Commas	**Developing Arguments 32** *Topic* How adults treat teenagers; Animal experiments *Language focus* Drafting and delivering speeches
Poetry *Topics* Shape poems; List poems; Recipe poems; Limericks; Performance poems	**Poetry** *Topics* Comparison poems *Language focus* Similes; Drafting	**Poetry 40** *Topics* Ballads; Raps *Language focus* Accent and dialect; Drafting
Storytelling *Topic* Ghost stories *Language focus* Paragraphs; Plots	**Storytelling** *Topics* UFOs; Science-fiction stories *Language focus* Punctuation	**Storytelling 50** *Topic* Describing characters; Dialogue *Language focus* Punctuation; Drafting
Stories from the Past *Topics* Myths and legends *Language focus* Library skills; Dictionary skills	**Stories from the Past** *Topics* The Canterbury Tales; An Indian folk tale; An American story and poem *Language focus* The development of the English language; Dictionary skills	**Stories from the Past 60** *Topic* Shakespeare's Macbeth *Language focus* The development of the English language
Media Texts *Topics* Comics; Graphic novels *Language focus* Exclamation marks; Spelling	**Media Texts** *Topic* Magazines *Language focus* IT skills	**Media Texts 70** *Topic* Newspapers *Language focus* IT skills
Persuading *Topics* Safety leaflets; Cautionary tales *Language focus* Spelling *Language focus* Nouns; Verbs	**Persuading** *Topic* Advertising *Language focus* Adjectives; Spelling	**Persuading 80** *Topic* Holiday brochures and leaflets *Language focus* Punctuation; Conjunctions
Scripts and Scriptwriting *Topics* Playscripts; Radio scripts *Language focus* Accents and dialects	**Scripts and Scriptwriting** *Topic* From script to stage *Language focus* Dialects	**Scripts and Scriptwriting 88** *Topic* Soap operas *Language focus* Register; Slang

The units Each unit looks at a particular way in which language is used. For example, in the first unit ('Personal Writing') you will be looking at how language is used to write diaries. You will be reading some diary entries and writing diary entries of your own.

Each unit is divided into short chapters, which deal with different topics. For example, the first chapter in the book is called 'Keeping a Diary'.

The chapters also contain several different kinds of activity, which will help you to develop your basic skills in English. The boxes on the rest of this page tell you more about these activities, and give you some advice about how to do them.

To the Student

Speaking and Listening

There are a variety of speaking and listening activities, including story-telling, role-plays and making tape-recordings, as well as discussions. These will help you to develop your ability to speak confidently in various situations.

- Take turns to speak.
- Remember to listen carefully when others are speaking.
- When it is your turn, make sure you speak clearly.

Reading

You will be reading all kinds of material, such as short stories, play scripts, poems and letters. The reading activities will help you to develop your ability to read with understanding.

- Read the passages slowly and carefully.
- If you don't understand any words, don't give up: they may become clear later. (Or you can ask your teacher for help.)
- Look at the pictures: they may help you understand what is going on.

Writing

The writing activities will help you to learn how to express yourself well. You will be trying different kinds of writing, such as film scripts, arguments and rap poems. You will also have the chance to design leaflets, storyboards and newspapers.

- Think about the question or topic before you start writing.
- If you are answering questions on a passage in the book, look back over the passage carefully before you write.
- When you have finished, re-read what you have written, and correct any mistakes.

Other Activities

- Several activities in this book will help you to improve your grammar, punctuation and spelling.
- Some units have activities that will help you to practise your dictionary skills, and to use a word processor and desk-top publishing programs.
- Other activities include holding a debate, creating a soap opera and performing scenes from a play.

A diary is a personal record of your experiences and your feelings. You can include anything – from what you think about this week's Number One CD, to your thoughts and feelings about your friends and enemies, your teachers and your parents. You can write detailed accounts of events you have enjoyed or brief notes about what you did during the day.

Keeping a Diary

Why Do People Keep Diaries?

Three young people explain why keeping a diary is important to them:

66 I use my diary to keep a record of things that I want to be able to remember. I don't write in it every day, but if something sad or exciting happens I always find time to write down how I feel about what's happened. **99**
Rosaline

66 I write something in my diary every day. If I'm having problems, it helps me to sort out what I feel about people and things. Keeping a diary is like having a best friend that you can talk to whenever you've got something on your mind. **99**
Wallace

66 Although my diary is very personal, I don't mind my close friends reading it. I don't write anything about anybody that I wouldn't mind them seeing. I don't write in it regularly, just when I'm feeling in the mood. **99**
Jasreen

Famous Diaries

People have kept diaries for thousands of years. Some of the most famous diaries are those kept by **Samuel Pepys** between 1660 and 1669. They tell us what life was like in London during the Great Plague in 1665 and the Great Fire of London in 1666.

Another famous diary is the diary kept by a young Jewish girl called **Anne Frank**. Her diary tells us what it was like to live in Holland, hiding from the Nazis during World War Two (1939–1945).

Speaking and Listening

- In groups, discuss what you learn from this page about diaries.
- What sort of things do the three young people write about in their diaries? What different reasons do they give to explain why keeping a diary is important to them?
- Have you ever kept a diary? How often did you write in your diary? What sort of things did you write about? If you have stopped keeping it, why did you stop?

The Secret Diary of a Teacher

The following extracts are from the diary of Jennifer Fryer, BA, aged 26-and-a-half.

Monday 21st

I overslept because I was tired from having had such a great weekend, and I was almost late. 9K seemed to have the Monday morning blues. It was impossible to get them to concentrate. Johnny Callaghan is a real nuisance. He just won't stop talking, so I gave him another detention.

Must remember Auntie Vi's birthday on Wednesday.

Wednesday 23rd

A dreadful day. 9K played up all lesson. Jason Phipps got hold of Sandra Vincent's hairspray and started squirting it everywhere. I kept ten of them in at break.

I forgot to send Auntie Vi a present, so I had to ring her up. I've spent most of the evening on the phone, listening to her rabbiting on, instead of doing my marking.

Tuesday 22nd

I got a letter from Kevin asking me to go windsurfing in Cornwall at Easter. I'd love to go windsurfing again, but I'm not sure I could stand going with Kevin.

I came home with a headache. It's that group in 10G. They're so noisy and difficult. I wish I didn't have them last thing in the afternoon.

Speaking and Listening

Read the extracts from Jennifer Fryer's diary. On your own, make notes of your answers to the following questions, then share your ideas in a group discussion.

- What impression do you get of her from these entries?
- What do you think she looks like?
- What clothes do you think she wears?
- Where do you think she lives?
- How do you think she travels to school?
- What sort of teacher do you think she is?
- Would you like to be in one of her classes or have her as a form tutor?

Writing

- Imagine you are Jennifer Fryer. Write the entries that she made in her diary for the Thursday and Friday of that week.
- *Either* invent your own teacher and write some entries for their secret diary, *or* write entries for the secret diary of one of these teachers: **a** Arthur Cainemall, aged 55; **b** Doreen Dontmesswithme, aged 40; or **c** Benjamin Bookworm, aged 28.
- Write some entries for *The Secret Diary of a Parent*.

Zlata's Diary

Zlata Filipović was living in Yugoslavia in a town called Sarajevo when civil war broke out in her country. She kept a diary describing what it was like to live there during the fighting.

She called her diary Mimmy. Here is an extract from it.

Sunday, 14 June 1992

Dear Mimmy,

There's still no electricity, so we're still cooking on the stove in the yard. Around 14.00, when we were doing something around the stove, a shell fell on the opposite corner of the street, destroying Zoka's wonderful jewellery shop. We ran straight to the cellar, waiting for the barrage. Luckily there was only that one shell, so we went back at around 16.00.

Your Zlata

Tuesday, 16 June 1992

Dear Mimmy,

Our windows are broken. All of them except the ones in my room. That's the result of the revolting shell that fell again on Zoka's jewellery shop, across the way from us. I was alone in the house at the time. Mummy and Daddy were down in the yard, getting lunch ready, and I had gone upstairs to set the table. Suddenly I heard a terrible bang and glass breaking. I was terrified and ran towards the hall. That same moment, Mummy and Daddy were at the door. Out of breath, worried, sweating and pale they hugged me and we ran to the cellar, because the shells usually come one after the other. When I realised what had happened, I started to cry and shake. Everybody tried to calm me down, but I was very upset. I barely managed to pull myself together.

We returned to the flat to find the rooms full of glass and the windows broken. We cleared away the glass and put plastic sheeting over the windows. We had had a close shave with that shell and shrapnel. I picked up a piece of shrapnel and the tail end of a grenade, put them in a box and thanked God I had been in the kitchen, because I could have been hit ... HORRIBLE! I don't know how often I've written that word. HORRIBLE. We've had too much horror. The days here are full of horror. Maybe we in Sarajevo could rename the day and call it horror, because that's really what it's like.

Love, Zlata

Reading and Writing

Read the two entries from Zlata's diary (page 8). Now answer these questions by choosing the correct answer from the three answers given at the end of each sentence. Then copy out the correct sentence.

1 Cooking was difficult for Zlata's family because **a** they had no fuel **b** there was no electricity **c** the stove was broken.

2 On Sunday a shell fell opposite Zlata's house and destroyed **a** a jeweller's shop **b** a furniture shop **c** a clothes shop.

3 On Sunday afternoon Zlata and her family hid in **a** the attic **b** the garage **c** the cellar.

4 Another shell hit the shop opposite on **a** Monday **b** Tuesday **c** Wednesday.

5 The shell went off while Zlata was **a** setting the table **b** doing the washing up **c** cleaning the flat.

6 Zlata's parents rushed upstairs **a** to clear up the mess **b** to see if Zlata was alright **c** to give Zlata first aid.

7 In the cellar Zlata started **a** to laugh and giggle **b** to shout and scream **c** to cry and shake.

8 Zlata and her parents repaired the windows with **a** plastic sheeting **b** wooden boards **c** new panes of glass.

9 In the flat Zlata found **a** two empty cartridge cases **b** a bullet and a piece of shrapnel **c** the tail end of a grenade and a piece of shrapnel.

10 The diary entries tell us that Zlata **a** found the war exciting **b** hated the war **c** didn't mind the war.

Writing

- Imagine that you were at home when a terrorist bomb exploded outside your house. Write a diary entry, like Zlata's, describing the explosion and your thoughts and feelings about it.

- Write a diary entry describing a day you'll never forget, because something dramatic happened. It could be something that happened to someone in your family, to your friends or at your school, or it could be a day when you heard some dramatic news. Before you begin, read what Tracy wrote in her diary (right) on the day she learned that Diana, Princess of Wales had been killed in a car crash.

A day I'll never forget

Today everyone's in a state of shock. I'd had a lie-in, because it's Sunday. I was in the bathroom when I heard my sister shouting something. She'd just switched the TV on and heard the news. None of us could believe it at first. It took a long time for it to sink in that she really was dead. Mum kept saying: 'How awful! It's those two poor boys that I feel sorry for.' After lunch we went round to Gran's as usual. Everyone kept talking about it all day.

Writing Your Own Diary

Rees Morgan lives on a farm in a village near Haverfordwest in Wales. Here are two entries from his diary.

Saturday 20 March 1999

I'm helping Dad and Grandad. We're lambing at the moment. My arms ache because I've been helping to carry sheep into the lambing shed most of the day. Grandad gave me £20 so I'll be able to buy two new CDs.

I got a letter from cousin Geraint this morning. They are settled into their new house in Swansea and he's asked me to go there during the Easter holidays. I hope Mum will let me go.

Sunday 21 March 1999

Great news! Mum says I can go to stay with cousin Geraint. It'll be fantastic. There's lots more to do in Swansea than there is here.

I spent the afternoon doing my homework, then watched the rugby highlights.

Clem is ill. We wonder if he's eaten something poisonous. He's a good sheepdog and I'm really worried that it's serious. I'm scared he might die. Dad says if he's not better by the morning, he'll get the vet.

Speaking and Listening

In groups, study the entries from Rees's diary and discuss these questions. Choose someone to make notes of your answers, then share your ideas in a class discussion.

- What do you learn about how he spent the weekend?
- What do the entries tell you about **a** his interests, **b** his thoughts and feelings?
- What sort of person do you think Rees is? Does he seem to be the kind of person who would make a good friend? Give reasons for your views.
- Imagine you are historians living in 2099. Make a list of the facts you would learn from reading Rees's diary about what life was like for a young boy living in a Welsh village in 1999.

Writing

Write at least two entries for a diary of your own. Write entries for either last weekend or the last few days. Before you begin, read the list of hints on how to write diary entries.

How to Write Diary Entries

1 Don't try to write about every single thing that happened during the day. Look back at Rees's entries and notice how each day he focused on two or three things that were important to him. Choose two or three important things that happened during the day and focus on them.

2 Put in lots of details – especially about your thoughts and feelings. Try to write a paragraph about each subject or incident you have chosen. If it's a very special day, such as a birthday or celebration, you might want to write several paragraphs. For example, Vaneta wrote several paragraphs in her diary about her family celebrating Divali (see below).

3 Because diaries are a personal form of writing, you can **write in a very informal style**. Your writing can be conversational and chatty. Notice how Rees includes exclamations like 'Great news!' Treat your diary as if it is a friend and you are talking directly to it.

4 Take as much care with the **grammar, spelling and punctuation** of your diary entries as you would with any other piece of writing. If you don't take care with everything you write, you can get into the habit of making careless mistakes!

Today we celebrated Divali. I got up early, so that I'd have plenty of time to have a bath before we went to the temple. Afterwards we went round to my cousin's house.

They had decorated their house in the traditional way and drawn some rangoli on the floor. We talked and danced round the patterns and pictures of flowers and animals, while my younger brothers played games. Then we had the food. It was delicious – especially all the different sweets!

When it started to get dark we lit all the candles to light up the windows and we danced some more. Then we went outside for the fireworks. Luckily it wasn't raining and we had a great time.

Tomorrow is our New Year's Day. I wonder what presents I'll get.

Prefixes and Suffixes

Prefixes

Many words are made up of more than one part.

For example, the word *unfair* is made up of two parts – *un* and *fair*.

A group of letters that is added in front of a word, to make a new word is called a **prefix**.

The prefix *un* means 'not'. When you add the prefix *un* to a word, it makes a new word with the opposite or negative meaning. Here are some more examples:

un + kind = unkind (not kind)

un + pleasant = unpleasant (not pleasant)

un + certain = uncertain (not certain).

There are other prefixes that mean 'not'. Look at the table on the right.

Prefix	Example	Meaning
dis	dis + obedient	disobedient (not obedient)
il	il + legal	illegal (not legal)
im	im + perfect	imperfect (not perfect)
in	in + accurate	inaccurate (not accurate)
ir	ir + regular	irregular (not regular)

Note: When you add a negative prefix, you do not change the spelling of the original word.

Take Responsibility for Your Spelling

- A lot of spelling mistakes are the result of carelessness. Before you hand in your work, always check your spellings carefully. If you are unsure about a word, use a dictionary to find the correct spelling.

- Keep a spelling book. When your teacher shows you that you have made a spelling mistake, write out the correct spelling in your spelling book.

- Spend some time each week learning your spellings. Use the Look-Focus-Say-Cover-Write-Check method to help you learn your spellings (see *English Direct 1*, page 21).

Writing

Look at the sentences below. The words in the brackets need to be changed to their opposite meanings by adding one of these negative prefixes: *un*, *dis*, *il*, *im*, *in* or *ir*. Choose the right prefix for the word in the brackets and copy out the sentence. The first one has been done for you.

1 When there is a long queue, people often get (patient).

When there is a long queue, people often get impatient.

2 She came last in the race because she was (fit).

3 The teacher put a cross because the answer was (correct).

4 The magician made the rabbit (appear).

5 A person who tells lies is (honest).

6 Driving a car without a licence is (responsible).

7 Clothes that are cheap are (expensive).

8 Your writing is so (legible) that I cannot read it.

Suffixes

An **adjective** is a word that tells you more about a noun. For example, in the sentence 'The bright sun shone', the word <u>bright</u> is an adjective.

An **adverb** is a word that tells you more about a verb. For example, in the sentence 'The sun was shining brightly', the word <u>brightly</u> is an adverb.

Many adjectives can be changed into adverbs by adding the letters *ly* at the end. For example:

bright (adjective) + *ly* = *brightly* (adverb)

quiet (adjective) + *ly* = *quietly* (adverb).

A group of letters that is added to the end of a word to make a new word is called a **suffix**.

Turning Adjectives into Adverbs

In many cases, an adverb is formed by adding the suffix <u>ly</u> without changing the spelling of the original word. However, there are some exceptions.

- There are a number of words that have two or more syllables and end in <u>y</u>. For example:

  happy, lazy, easy.

  To make these words into adverbs you cut off the <u>y</u> and add <u>ily</u>:

  happy ▶ *happ* ▶ *happily*

  lazy ▶ *laz* ▶ *lazily*

  easy ▶ *eas* ▶ *easily*.

- However, if the word has only one syllable and ends in *y*, you usually form the adverb by adding <u>ly</u>. For example:

  shy + *ly* ▶ *shyly*.

- There are a few words, such as *dull* and *full*, that end with *ll*. These words add <u>y</u> only. For example:

  dull ▶ *dully*

  full ▶ *fully*.

Writing

Read the following passage. The words in the brackets are adjectives, which need to be changed into adverbs in order for the passage to make sense. Copy out the passage and add the right suffix to each of the adjectives so that it becomes an adverb.

The waves were lapping (calm) against the beach and the sun was shining (bright). Some people were lying (lazy) on the sand, while others were splashing (happy) in the sea. A motor boat sped (swift) across the bay. A seagull pecked (hungry) at the remains of a sandwich, and a donkey plodded (slow) along, giving rides. Music blared (loud) from a radio as a group of teenagers walked along the promenade chatting (cheerful).

HOW TO MAKE A COMPLAINT

If you want to complain about an item you've bought, you don't have to contact the manufacturer. It's up to the person who sold it to you to sort it out.

If you broke the item by using it carelessly, then you haven't really got a case for complaining. But if the item won't work properly, or doesn't do what it was claimed to do, then take it back to the shop that sold it to you.

If you feel you have a genuine complaint, then contact the seller. The three ways you can do this are listed on the right.

Whether you write, telephone or go into the shop, always be polite. If necessary, keep repeating why you are complaining, but keep calm and do not raise your voice.

1 By going into the store or shop
- Stop using the item and take it back to the store or shop that it came from.
- Take either a receipt or proof of purchase with you, if you have got one.
- When you go in, ask to see a senior member of staff, such as a supervisor or the manager.

2 By writing a letter
If you have a difficult problem, it may be better to write to the firm's manager or managing director.
- State clearly where and when you bought the item and what the problem is.
- Keep a copy of the letter.
- Don't enclose your receipt or proof of purchase. Either quote the reference number or send a photocopy.
- Send the letter by recorded delivery to ensure that it gets there.

3 By telephoning
- Plan carefully what you are going to say before you pick up the phone. It can be useful to make a list of the points you want to make.
- Make sure you ask for the name of the person you speak to. You might need it later, if the problem doesn't get sorted out quickly.
- Keep a record of the conversation. Note down the date and the time and what was said.

Getting further advice

If you complain to the seller and they are unable or unwilling to sort the problem out, then ask a consumer adviser for advice. You can contact either a Citizens Advice Bureau, Consumer Advice Centre or Trading Standards Department. You can find their addresses and telephone numbers in the telephone directory.

Sometimes, the problem isn't solved either by contacting the seller or with the help of a consumer adviser. If you can't solve the problem in any other way, you may have to go to court to ask for compensation. Whether or not it is worth the trouble and expense will depend on the size of your claim.

Reading and Writing

Read the leaflet 'How to Make a Complaint' (page 14), then write sentences in answer to these questions.

1 If you have a complaint about an item, who should you take it up with?

2 What are the two genuine reasons for complaining about an item you have bought?

3 When you go in to make a complaint, who should you ask to see?

4 What three pieces of information should a letter of complaint contain?

5 Suggest the reasons why you are advised: **a** to keep a copy of the letter you send; **b** not to send the receipt.

6 Which of the pieces of advice about how to make a complaint by telephone do you think is the most important? Give your reasons.

7 What advice are you given about how to behave when making a complaint over the telephone or in a store?

8 What is the last step you can take, if you cannot reach agreement in any other way?

Speaking and Listening

In pairs, role-play the following scenes, in which a person makes a complaint about an item they have purchased. Repeat the scene twice, taking it in turns to be the customer.

- A teenager takes something that they bought for their bicycle back to the cycle shop because it doesn't work properly.

- A customer takes a personal stereo back to the shop they bought it from because it distorts the sound of the music they try to play.

Drawing and Writing

Draw picture strips to show: **a** the wrong way to go about making a complaint about a faulty item; **b** the right way to make a complaint.

In the first picture strip show Cheeky Clementine being rude and aggressive. In the second picture strip show how Martin Good-Manners explains his problem calmly and politely, so that it is quickly solved.

Writing a Letter of Complaint

Put the date under the address of the person you are writing to.

Put your own address in the top right-hand corner.

Put the name and address of the person you are writing to on the left.

Start 'Dear Sir/Madam', unless you know the manager's name.

Leave a gap between the margin and the first word of a paragraph.

Start a new paragraph on a new line.

End 'Yours faithfully', unless you know the person's name. If you do know it, end 'Yours sincerely'.

Sign your name here.

Write your name in capitals underneath your signature.

```
The Manager,                              40 Mulberry Way,
Super Shirts,                             Froghampton,
Baskington,                               Loamshire
Loamshire                                 LM22 6ST
LM8 3ET

28 May 1999

Dear Sir/Madam
    I purchased a patterned T-shirt with a print of
the pop group 'Overexcited' on it for £10.99 at your
Froghampton branch on Saturday 19 May. I enclose a
copy of my receipt.

    Your assistant assured me that it would fit as it
was a new 'skin-tight' type suitable for all sizes.
However, the shirt has come away at the stitching
under the arms. Another problem is that the print
has blurred. I have only worn the shirt once and it
has had one hand wash.

    I took the shirt back to the Froghampton store
but the assistant refused to change it, because she
said it had been worn and washed. I would like
either a replacement shirt that will fit me properly
or to have a refund.

Yours faithfully

    Kirsty Higgs
KIRSTY HIGGS
```

Writing

Imagine that you bought a pair of BettaFit shoes for £16.99 from Smartyfeet plc, 23 High Street, Yortown YO6 7PN on 14 November 1999. Within ten days the heels came off and the seams split. You took the shoes back and the manager, Mrs Jenkins, offered to repair them, but refused to change them. Write a letter to the Managing Director, Smartyfeet plc, Footwear House, Soledby SO6 2YN.

In the first paragraph, state what type of shoes they are, where and when you bought them and how much you paid for them.

In the second paragraph, explain how they broke and what happened when you took them back to the shop.

In the third paragraph, ask either for a refund or your money back.

Before you begin, study the letter above. Make sure you lay your letter out properly, putting the name and address of the person to whom you are writing, the date and your own address in the correct positions, and that you start and end your letter in the proper way.

Sentences and Paragraphs

Writing

Here is Kelly's draft of a letter complaining about a bag she bought. Unfortunately, it is difficult to read because she has forgotten to use full stops and capital letters. Copy it out and correct it by putting in punctuation marks.

i bought a new holdall from the west street branch of bargains galore in chiddleberry on the afternoon of saturday 25 august 1999 the holdall was a black karry-a-lot which was advertised as especially suitable for students and cost me £15.99 the salesman had to get one from the back of the store, because there were no black ones on the shelves

when i got home, i unpacked the holdall and found it was damaged there is a large scratch on one side also, the zip is broken i took the holdall back to the west street branch and asked for it to be exchanged the person i spoke to was the manager, mrs proud she said I must have damaged it myself and refused either to exchange it or to give me a refund i left the holdall at the store, because I did not want to be falsely accused of damaging it any further

i am writing to ask for either a replacement or a refund, because the holdall i was sold was faulty i enclose a copy of the receipt i would be grateful if you could give this matter your immediate attention, as i need a holdall for when school starts next week

Remember:

● A **sentence** is something written or spoken that makes sense. It usually consists of several words.
● A sentence always begins with a *capital letter*, and must end with either a *full stop*, a *question mark* or an *exclamation mark*.

Remember:

● A **paragraph** is a group of sentences, all of which are about the same idea or subject.
● Writers do two things to show where a new paragraph starts:
1 They start the first sentence of a new paragraph on a new line.
2 They *either* leave a space between the margin (the edge of the page) and the first word of a new paragraph, *or* they leave a blank line, known as a line space, between paragraphs.

Speaking and Listening

In pairs, look at Kelly's letter. How many paragraphs are there in it? Discuss what each paragraph is about.

Martin Luther King
– A factsheet

- Martin Luther King was born in America in 1929. As a boy, he was not allowed to use the same toilet, park, cinema or library as a white person. Because his family was black, they had to live in a poor area for black people only. He grew up hating the unfairness of the system called segregation, which kept black people and white people apart.

- Martin was clever and he went to a college for black students when he was only fifteen years old. He made up his mind to become a church minister. At college, he also decided that he would join the civil rights movement and help black Americans fight for their civil rights. He was determined to do so without using violence.

- In 1953, he got married and became a church minister in the state of Alabama. Segregation was very strict in Alabama. Black people were only allowed to sit at the back of a bus. Martin Luther King organised a bus boycott. Black people said they wouldn't travel on buses until they could sit wherever they liked.

- The bus boycott lasted a year and the black people won. Because he had organised the protest, some white people hated Martin Luther King. He received about thirty hate letters every day and his house was bombed. This only made Martin more determined than ever to demand equal rights for black people.

- He organised marches and gave speeches. More and more people joined the campaign for black people's rights. In 1963, he planned a huge march to Washington, where he gave his famous speech 'I have a dream'. Here is an extract from that speech:

  ❝ I have a dream that my four little children will one day live in a nation where they will not be judged by the colour of their skin but by the content of their character. ❞

- Martin Luther King never gave up his campaign to win equal rights for black people. But he did not live to see his dream come true. On 4 April 1968 he was shot dead by a hired killer called James Earl Ray in Memphis. Ray never told anybody who hired him.

- When he was murdered, Martin Luther King was only thirty-nine years old. Today he is thought of as one of America's greatest men. His birthday is now a national holiday.

Reading and Writing

Read the factsheet on Martin Luther King, which Kenyon wrote after reading books and articles about him. Then write sentences in answer to these questions.

1 In what sort of area did Martin Luther King live as a child?

2 a Explain what segregation was.
   b State two things that black people could not do, because of segregation.

3 a At what age did Martin Luther King go to college?
   b What two things did he decide to do while he was at college?

4 a Where did he go to live after he got married?

   b Explain what a bus boycott is.
   c Why did Martin Luther King organise a bus boycott?
   d What was the result of the boycott?

5 a Why did some people send Martin Luther King hate letters?
   b What effect did the letters have on him?

6 a Where did he give his most famous speech?
   b What was his most famous speech called?

7 How did Martin Luther King die?

8 Why is Martin Luther King's birthday a national holiday in America?

Research and Writing

Choose a famous person (either living or dead) and produce your own factsheet of them, similar to Kenyon's factsheet of Martin Luther King. Prepare your factsheet in stages.

Stage 1 Find out as much as you can about the person you have chosen by looking them up in books and on CD-ROMs in the school library and local library.

Stage 2 Make notes of what you learn about them under different headings, for example:
• where and when they were born;
• childhood and education;
• achievements.

Stage 3 Plan your factsheet by deciding what you are going to put in each paragraph. Draw up a paragraph plan like the one Kenyon drew:

Paragraph 1 – Birth and childhood.
Paragraph 2 – At college – Decided to become a minister. Joined civil rights movement.
Paragraph 3 – Went to live in Alabama. Organised bus boycott.
Paragraph 4 – Became a hated figure.
Paragraph 5 – Organised Washington march. Gave 'I have a dream' speech.
Paragraph 6 – Murdered.
Paragraph 7 – Became a national hero.

Stage 4 Draft your factsheet. As you do so, be prepared to change your paragraph plan, if you find you have either too much information or too little information for any particular paragraph.

Stage 5 Design a layout for your factsheet. If possible, use a desk-top publishing package and experiment with different layouts until you find a suitable one for your article.

Stage 6 Either print out or write out a neat copy of your factsheet.

The Police and You

Being Stopped and Searched

The police have a lot of power, but there are legal restrictions on their powers to stop and search you.

Being stopped

The police can stop you and ask for your name and address. They can ask you where you are going and where you have been. This is most likely to happen late at night.

Being searched

The police do not have a general power to search you. But they can search you or your bag if they have reasonable grounds for suspecting they will find you in possession of stolen or prohibited articles. For example, they can search you if they think you are carrying a knife, or something that might be used to hurt someone, for example a broken bottle. You can also be searched if they think you have got drugs on you, or if you are travelling to and from a football match and they believe you have alcohol with you.

If you are searched, keep calm. If you start shouting and swearing and either struggle with or threaten the police, you might commit an offence for which you could be charged.

Information can often be made more interesting if it is presented in a lively way. Farhan and Stephanie were both given the same information and asked to produce leaflets about police powers to stop and search. Farhan presented the information as a leaflet (above). Stephanie decided to present the information as a cartoon strip. Here is the start of her cartoon.

The police can stop you and ask you where you've been.

The police can search you if they think you are carrying stolen goods.

Writing and Drawing

- Draw the other pictures that Stephanie might have drawn in her cartoon strip and write captions for them.

- Study the information about arrests on page 21. Design a page that presents the same information in a more lively way.

Arrests

If you have committed a road traffic offence or a minor criminal offence (for example not paying your fare on public transport) and the police are satisfied without needing to make any further investigations that you are guilty, they will take your name and address and you may subsequently receive a *summons (see further Chapter 16, Criminal Proceedings, heading (c))*.

If you are suspected of a more serious criminal offence and the police wish to make further investigations, it is likely that they will arrest you.

The police do not have a general power to arrest you.

They can arrest you with a warrant, which is a written authority from a magistrate, but they can also arrest you without a warrant in certain circumstances.

The main circumstances are that they have reasonable grounds for suspecting you of having committed, or being in the act of committing, or being about to commit an *arrestable offence*. Arrestable offences include

- all *serious* offences such as murder, rape, robbery, burglary, theft and assault and offences in relation to controlled drugs;

- other less serious offences such as violent disorder, causing criminal damage, indecent assault, taking a motor vehicle without the owner's consent, driving while disqualified and going equipped for burglary, theft or cheat.

There are further powers of arrest for

- affray and threatening behaviour and also disorderly conduct if you carry on after having being warned to stop (*see generally Chapter 41, Public Order Offences*);
- drink driving;
- having alcohol with you at a league or cup football match or on a coach or train travelling to or from such a match.

You can be arrested if you are actually breaching the peace or acting in such a way that a breach of the peace is likely to occur.

You can be arrested for non-arrestable offences, such as indecent exposure, carrying a bladed or sharply pointed article (for example a pen knife with a blade of more than 7.5 cm in length) and not paying your fare on public transport if

- you refuse to give your name and address, or give false details; *or*
- you do not have a permanent address so that you can be *summoned*; *or*
- in order to prevent you from
  - causing injury to yourself or others; *or*
  - causing loss of or damage to any property; *or*
  - committing an offence against public decency; *or*
  - obstructing the highway.

In this unit you will be talking about what makes a good story and discussing the types of stories you like to read. You will be reading and writing book reviews and writing in detail about a book you have read. You will also be reading and writing reviews of computer games.

What Makes a Good Story?

Here are some people talking about what makes a good story.

'The ideal story takes hold of the reader in a second and stays with them for years ... The best stories are told simply. Not words of one syllable, but the right words, the needful words, none wasted, none getting in the way of the reader. The more vivid the picture, the more real the action, the more *point* to what happens, the longer the story will stay in the memory.'
– Robert Leeson, children's writer

'A good story is like a puzzle. It leaves you guessing, so you want to find out what happens. And the best stories always have a twist in them. Something unexpected happens to surprise you.'
– Anya, student

'Good stories have got interesting characters in them, but also ones that you can identify with. You need to be able to see life through the eyes of the characters, however extraordinary they are.'
– Anya's parent

'There's got to be plenty of action in them. Good stories are fast-moving. There is plenty going on. They're not full of boring descriptions.'
– Sanjay, student

'A good story is one that moves you in some way. It makes you laugh or cry – or scares you silly! A good story also teaches you something about life. You feel as if you've learned something from it.'
– Sanjay's teacher

In Groups

- Discuss each of the comments in turn and say whether you agree or disagree with it.
- What do you think makes a good story? Each write down one thing that you think is important in a good story. Then discuss what you have written.
- Make a list of all the things that people in your group think make a good story. Then appoint someone to act as spokesperson and share your ideas in a class discussion.

The Stories I Like

Here is a list of different types of story. Write out the list in alphabetical order and then put a circle round the type of story that you like best.

horror animal historical thriller family science fiction Western ghost romance sport fantasy

Now do a class survey to find out which kinds of story other people in the class like. Make a chart like the one class 11BD made (on the right).

Below, Magda and Karl are writing about the type of story they like best.

Our favourite type of story										
Sport	X	X	X	X	X	X				
Romance	X	X	X	X						
Horror	X	X	X	X	X	X	X	X	X	X
Science fiction	X	X								
Ghost	X	X	X	X						
Animal	X									

I like reading photo love stories. The stories tell you about real-life situations, so you can identify with the characters. There are no boring descriptions to read, because you can see what the people are like in the pictures. If the story is a serial in a magazine, you have to wait until next week to find out what happens. It makes you think about what you would do if you fancied someone and they treated you like that.

Magda

My favourite stories are supernatural stories. I read them because I like being scared. I particularly like the descriptions of strange creatures like werewolves and other supernatural beings. The stories have lots of action in them and some of the things that happen are really weird.

Karl

Writing

Read what Magda and Karl wrote about the stories they like, then write a paragraph about the type of stories you like.

Remember to write proper sentences, starting each one with a capital letter and ending each one with a full stop.

BOOK REVIEWS

The Other Side of the Fence
by Jean Ure

This book is about Richard, a withdrawn college student who has everything except understanding. An argument with his father leaves him homeless. He then meets Bonny, a dreamer with a great imagination, trying to hitch a lift. They both go to London in search of a home and a job.

The Other Side of the Fence leaves you wondering 'could this happen to me?' It's a marvellous book and has made me want to read other books by Jean Ure.

David Fox, aged 14

Getting It Right by Lynne Markham

'My arm lifts up of its own accord, and my fist goes through the window. I can hear the slivers of glass clinking like ice-cubes as they clatter to the ground. There's a whiteness on my fist, and then red which spurts as if it won't ever stop.'

Peter's mother leaves him and he is sent to Norwell House. The Cox family finally take him in after he has been to stay with three other families. Angela Cox hates him; his friend, Anvil, the tramp, goes missing and Tyler is out to get him. Times are hard for Peter.

This is a very good book and shows you what it is like from both points of view – the family's as well as Peter's. It is emotional and dramatic and well worth reading. I would recommend it to anybody over the age of 13.

David Macklin, aged 14

Reading and Writing

On your own, study the reviews, then answer these questions.

1 Write down the title of the book you would recommend to:
   a a friend who likes supernatural stories;
   b a friend who likes stories about relationships;
   c a friend who likes stories with plenty of action;
   d a friend who likes mystery stories;
   e a friend who likes real-life stories.

(Note: You can recommend the same title more than once.)

2 Which book do you think would be:
   a the most interesting to read;
   b the least interesting to read?

Write a short statement, giving the reasons for your views.

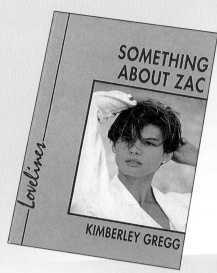

Aidan's Fate by Jesse Harris

McKenzie Gold can often sense things that other people can't. Also her dreams have a nasty habit of coming true. One night she dreams that her boyfriend, Aidan, is killed in a car-crash. From then on she is haunted by a mysterious ticking that no one else can hear and is convinced that time is running out for Aidan.

This book was good because it was very descriptive and made you feel that McKenzie's gift was something anyone could have.

Catherine Smith, aged 14

Something About Zac
by Kimberley Gregg

Marlee is a new girl in town and has just met a gorgeous boy called Zac. He is quite rich and very intelligent. Then one day he disappears, causing Marlee a lot of anxiety. Marlee forgives him because she is also having trouble at home. But when a boy starts to hit a girl it becomes serious.

I think that this book is good because it tells you about everyday life from a teenager's point of view. I rate it eight out of ten.

Mariam Malik, aged 13

Tasting the Thunder
by Gary Paulsen

This is an interesting book about a boy of sixteen who leaves home to find out about life the hard way and what it is like to be a man. He starts working for Karl on a beet field and soon discovers for himself how Karl beats up boys and old men. He runs away and joins the fairground people where he learns about their life and work. Then something terrible happens which he will never forget.

Mandip Samra, aged 14

Speaking and Listening

In groups, show each other what you have written. Discuss which books you recommended and why. Talk about which books you would most like to read and least like to read, and explain why.

Writing

Write a short review of a book you have read and enjoyed.

Plan your writing in paragraphs.

In your first paragraph, make sure you write something about each of the following:
- *the main characters* – who the people in the story are;
- *the setting* – where and when the story takes place;
- *the plot* – what happens in the story.

However, make sure you do not give away the ending of the story.

In your second paragraph, write three or four sentences saying why you liked the story and who you would recommend it to.

A Book Project

Lisa's class read *Buddy* by Nigel Hinton. The examples of what the class wrote are included in this chapter to help you to think closely about a book *you* have read, and to write your opinions about it.

NIGEL HINTON

Buddy

1 The book's title

- Why do you think the author gave it that title?
- Do you think it is a good title?
- Can you suggest an alternative title?

Give reasons for your views.

'Buddy' is an excellent title because it means 'friend'. The book mentions the singer Buddy Holly and the main character, Buddy Clark, is named after the dead singer. In the book Buddy has two good friends, Jules and Charmian.

An alternative title might be 'The Trouble with Dad', as the story is about the problems that Buddy has because of the way his dad dresses and behaves.

2 The beginning of the story

- Read the opening page of the story again. Think about how the story starts. Does it start with: **a** a description of a place; **b** a description of a person; **c** a dramatic event; **d** important background information; **e** a conversation; **f** in some other way?
- Did the opening capture your attention at once?
- Do you think it was a good way of starting the story?
- Can you suggest a different way that the story could have begun?

The opening captured my attention straight away, because in the first sentence Buddy stole money from his mother's purse. This is a very dramatic start. It was a good opening because it led to Buddy's mum and dad having a row. Buddy's mum left home and Buddy blamed himself.

It could have started after his mum had walked out, with Buddy thinking about what had happened. But I don't think that would have been as dramatic.

3 The plot

Make a list of the main events in the plot and draw either a time-line
or a flow-chart of the events in the order in which they happened.

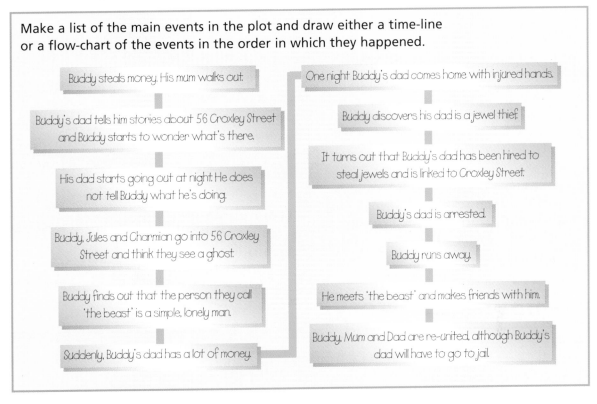

Buddy steals money. His mum walks out.

Buddy's dad tells him stories about 56 Croxley Street and Buddy starts to wonder what's there.

His dad starts going out at night. He does not tell Buddy what he's doing.

Buddy, Jules and Charmian go into 56 Croxley Street and think they see a ghost.

Buddy finds out that the person they call 'the beast' is a simple, lonely man.

Suddenly, Buddy's dad has a lot of money.

One night Buddy's dad comes home with injured hands.

Buddy discovers his dad is a jewel thief.

It turns out that Buddy's dad has been hired to steal jewels and is linked to Croxley Street.

Buddy's dad is arrested.

Buddy runs away.

He meets 'the beast' and makes friends with him.

Buddy, Mum and Dad are re-united, although Buddy's dad will have to go to jail.

4 The most exciting moment

- What was the most exciting moment in the story? Often this is a moment of suspense or tension, when you are not quite sure what is going to happen next. Sometimes it is a moment when you really feel involved and identify with the feelings a character is experiencing.
- Describe what happens at the most exciting moment in the story and say why you found it exciting.

> The most exciting moment in the story is when Buddy's dad is arrested. Buddy had tried to set up Mr King, but the police found Mr Clark and the simple man called Ralph James Campbell at Croxley Street. It is exciting because we are not sure what Buddy will do. All his plans have gone wrong and he now has nobody to look after him.

5 The characters

- Make a list of the main characters. What sort of people are they? Often the people in a story are changed in some way, because of the events that happen in a story.

- Which of the characters in the book is changed the most by the events of the story? In what way is the person changed?

- Write about the main characters in the book. Describe what sort of people they are and say which ones you like and which ones you don't like. Give reasons for your views.

Buddy's dad does not seem to change much, but that is the whole point of the story. He is stuck in a time warp, unable to change from the Buddy Holly era. He really annoyed me.

Buddy's mum married Terry Clark too young. I liked her because she is much more sensitive and she wants her independence. She wants to do the sort of things she missed when she was younger. She wants to make a career for herself.

Buddy is more like his mum than his dad and he is clever at school. Buddy changes, because he stops stealing and starts to understand things a bit more. I identified with Buddy.

6 Filming the story

- Imagine you were going to make a film of the story. Choose one of the key moments in the story and make a storyboard showing how you would film it.

Scene: Buddy, Jules and Charmian break into 56 Croxley Street

Buddy and his friends find a room with a camp bed in it. There are candles round the bed and some tins of food.

They look in another room and hear a sound. They turn round and come face to face with the man they call the Beast.

7 The ending

- How does the story end?
- Do you think it was a good ending? Give your reasons.
- How else could the story have ended?

Buddy's dad had to pay for his crimes and so his jail sentence was realistic. I did not like the fact that the real baddie, Mr King, got away with it, although Nigel Hinton does deal with Mr King in the sequel, 'Buddy's Song'.

I was glad Buddy's parents got together again. They would have a lot to sort out. Buddy's dad would have to accept his wife's wishes to be educated, and she would have to accept him for what he was. He doesn't seem to be capable of changing.

Computer Games

A review of a computer game is similar to a review of a book. A good review will tell you:

- the name of the game;
- what age-group the game is for;
- how to play it;
- how good the graphics and sound are;
- how much fun you'll get playing it.

Below are two reviews of computer games by Jason and Julia.

Bunny

Bunny is a game I played on my Amstrad computer. You become Bunny, who has to race along a maze of warrens picking up presents. If you run out of time before you collect 200 presents, you die.

However, there are clocks along the passages. If you reach a clock, you are given an extra minute. You can find yourself trapped in a warren with no clock, but there are keys you can pick up on the way.

I found the game exciting, because you do not know where the presents and clocks are. You suddenly find them there and you have to react quickly. But if you played the game a lot it might get boring. You'd start to know the different warrens.

Rating: *** Jason

Hypermaze

You are on a trip back to Earth for a holiday, when you hit a wormhole. Somehow you are transported straight to Earth. When you land you realise something is wrong. You are on a planet like Earth, but there are sorcerers, dragons and lots of other things to keep you puzzled.

This game will drag you to your PC every time you're in the same room. It is also well worth going through the optional introduction. The only problem is that it lasts 8 minutes!

This game is amazing. The only thing that lets it down is the sound, which can drive you crazy. Of course, you can just turn it off. The problem is you then can't hear the characters speaking, which can be quite a pain.

Rating: ***** Julia

Speaking and Listening

In pairs, discuss these questions.

- Which of the two games would you rather play – Bunny or Hypermaze? Explain why.
- Do Jason and Julia give you enough information about the games? What else would you like either of them to have told you about the game?

Writing

Write a review of a computer game that you have played. Explain how to play it and say whether you think it is exciting or boring. Use a five-star system to give it a rating (***** = excellent; * = poor).

The Comma

In *English Direct 2* (pages 68–69) you learned how to use **commas** to separate the words or phrases in a list. You also used commas to break up sentences. This chapter tells you more about using commas to break up sentences.

1 A comma is used when you want to show that there is a pause between two separate parts of a sentence. For example:

When Elizabeth opened the door, the room was empty.

The book was lying on the floor, so Jason picked it up.

Although I ran as fast as I could, Trevor still beat me.

2 Pairs of commas are used to mark off phrases in the middle of a sentence, which usually tell you more about the subject of a sentence. (The **subject** of a sentence is the person or thing doing the action described by the main verb in the sentence.) For example:

Roy Keane, the Manchester United midfield player, was sent off for two bookable offences.

Carmen, Nadia's sister, sang a solo in the concert.

Dennis, who had not been paying attention, was unable to answer the question.

The storm, which had been raging all night, caused lots of damage.

Writing

The commas in these sentences have been left out. Copy out the sentences and put in the missing commas.

1 After the dentist took her tooth out Teresa's mouth was sore.

2 Janice my elder sister is training to be a hairdresser.

3 The old man who lives at the end of the street refused to give us our ball back.

4 Although it was very cold we went for a walk on the beach.

5 When it is my birthday I am going to get a new pair of rollerblades.

6 The cat which I saw in the garden belongs to Mrs Spencer.

7 Rio Ferdinand the West Ham defender was one of the substitutes.

8 I asked my mum if I could go out but she said that I had to finish my homework first.

9 Martin Forbes the lead singer of the Silver Blades pop group slipped on the stage and broke his ankle.

10 While I was waiting for the bus Tracy Simpkins rode past.

Homophones

Some spelling mistakes occur because you use a word that means something different, although it sounds exactly the same as the word you meant to use. For example, Tim wrote:

I was fed up. I was really <u>board</u>.

What he should have written was:

I was fed up. I was really <u>bored</u>.

A word that sounds the same as another word, but has a different meaning and a different spelling, is called a **homophone**.

Writing

Copy out and complete the following sentences by choosing the correct homophone from the two in the brackets. Then use a dictionary to check that you have used the right one.

1 I wrote my name on a (peace piece) of paper.

2 You are not (allowed aloud) in there without permission.

3 I watched the next episode of the (serial cereal) on TV.

4 I don't know which dress to (wear where) to the party.

5 I cut my finger and it is very (saw sore).

6 They (tied tide) the prisoner up.

7 We watched the (plane plain) take off from the airport.

8 A square has (for four) sides.

9 You can (chews choose) a present to have on your birthday.

10 I mixed the eggs and (flower flour) in a bowl.

Using a Spellchecker

When you use a spellchecker on a word processor, you must always read through the passage afterwards to look for mistakes. This is because spellcheckers only pick out words that are actually misspelt. They will not pick out homophones.

In pairs, read the poem on the right. Find all the spelling mistakes in it and write out a correctly spelt version of it.

SPELLBOUND

I have a spelling chequer
It came with my PC
It plainly marks for my revue
Miss takes I cannot sea.
I've run this poem threw it
I'm shore your pleased to no;
It's letter perfect in its weigh
My chequer told me sew.
NORMAN VANDAL

Are Adults Fair to Teenagers?

Matt was asked to prepare a speech about the way adults treat teenagers. Here is his speech.

66 Do adults treat teenagers fairly? You must be joking! I don't know how we put up with them.

What's most unfair about adults is the way they are always complaining about us. They moan about our clothes, about our hairstyles and about our music. Surely it's up to us what we wear and what we want to listen to?

The worst thing about adults is the way they humiliate us and embarrass us in front of our friends. Last week, I took my new girlfriend home for the first time. Do you know what Mum did? She brought out a picture of me when I was a chubby two-year-old sitting in a paddling pool, holding a yellow plastic duck. I nearly died of embarrassment!

Another thing I can't stand is the way adults always think they're right. They never stop to listen to what you've got to say. My parents say I've got to be in at nine thirty on school days. But when I got home half an hour late last

Wednesday, because the bus never came, I was grounded for a week.

Why won't they ever listen to you?

Adults won't allow us to do things, then complain about the way we behave. They wouldn't let me go camping with my friends last summer. They said I was too young. Then when I was hanging round the house all day, bored because my friends were away, they kept complaining that I watched too much telly.

I don't think it's fair the way they keep on lecturing us.

If I'm going out to a party or anything like that, I always get a lecture about drugs – especially ecstasy, which I wouldn't touch anyway. Why can't they trust us?

Adults are crazy! They say they want us to grow up, then treat us like little children. If they treated us fairly, then maybe they'd find out just how grown up teenagers really are. 99

Speaking and Listening

- In groups, discuss Matt's speech (page 32). First, make a list of all the points he uses to support his argument that adults do not treat teenagers fairly. Then, say whether you agree or disagree with each point in turn, giving your reasons.

- Take it in turns to read Matt's speech aloud to the rest of the group. Decide whose reading was the most dramatic and discuss why.

Writing a Speech – The tricks of the trade

There are a number of things that you can do when writing a speech to help to make it effective.

1 Grab your listeners' attention

Make sure you start your speech in a way that will grab your listeners' attention.

For example, Matt could have begun his speech with a simple statement, such as: 'I do not think adults treat teenagers fairly.' Instead he sets out to grab his listeners' attention with a dramatic question and answer: 'Do adults treat teenagers fairly? You must be joking!'

2 Speak to the audience directly

This helps to get them on your side.

Notice how Matt says: 'I don't know how we put up with them.' Throughout the speech he refers to 'us'. This involves the audience by suggesting that it's not just Matt himself who is being unfairly treated, but any young people listening to him.

3 Include questions

These can have a dramatic effect, especially if they are questions that do not require an answer. This type of question is called a **rhetorical question**.

For example, Matt asks: 'Surely it's up to us what we wear and what we want to listen to?'

4 Include lists of three

If you list things in threes, it can help to hold your listeners' attention. They are also more likely to remember lists of three.

Matt uses a list of three when he says: 'They moan about our clothes, about our hairstyles and about our music.'

5 Use personal experiences

This suggests you really know what you are talking about.

Throughout his speech, Matt backs up his arguments with examples drawn from his own experience. For example, he uses the story of the photograph to show how adults can embarrass teenagers.

6 End dramatically

Make sure you end your speech on a high note. If you have a dramatic ending, your listeners are more likely to remember your argument

For example, Matt starts the final part of his speech with the dramatic statement: 'Adults are crazy!'

Drafting Your Own Speech

When you are preparing a speech, you should do it in stages. Here is how Nazrul planned a speech in which he presented his views on how animals are treated.

Stage 1: Finding the facts

Nazrul went to the library to look for information to support his view that people treat animals cruelly.

Before he went to the library, he asked his teacher if he knew of any useful books on the subject. His teacher recommended *What's the Big Idea? Animal Rights* by Anita Ganeri.

Nazrul also made a list of the subjects that he wanted to find out about. Here is his list.

Bull fighting
Battery hens
Foxhunting
Pets
Animal experiments
Zoos

Nazrul looked up 'Ganeri' in the author catalogue. He found that the library had a copy of *What's the Big Idea? Animal Rights*.

He also looked up 'Animals' in the subject catalogue and found that there were two other books on animal rights: *Survival: Animal Rights* by Miles Barton, and *The Young Person's Action Guide to Animal Rights* by Barbara James.

Nazrul arranged to take the three books out, then he looked for information on the subjects on his list in an encyclopedia on a CD-ROM.

The library also had a file of articles on animal issues from newspapers and magazines. So Nazrul looked in that too.

Nazrul took notes whenever he found any information that he thought he might use in his speech. Below are the notes he made about keeping pet rabbits in cages.

Rabbits live up to 14 years in the wild – only 7 in captivity. Wild rabbits live in families in burrows. They enjoy running round.

Pet rabbits live in small cages, often alone.

They don't get enough exercise.

Pet rabbits show signs of old age after about 5 years.

In one of the books, Nazrul found a list of addresses. So he wrote to the RSPCA and the League Against Cruel Sports and asked them if they could send him any leaflets about cruelty to animals.

Stage 2: Making a plan

Once Nazrul had gathered all the information, he read through his notes. He decided which pieces of information he was going to include in his speech, and he drew a flow-chart (below). Making a flow-chart helped him to plan the order in which he was going to put his ideas.

1 Opening
- The different types of cruelty to animals.

2 Cruelty of pet owners
- Keeping rabbits and birds in cages.
- RSPCA cases of cruelty to dogs and cats.

3 Cruelty on farms
- Battery hens.

4 Cruel sports
- Foxhunting, bull fighting, badger baiting.

5 Animals in zoos
- Animals should be free, not caged.

6 Animal testing
- Unnecessary suffering.

7 Circuses
- Animals shouldn't be made to perform tricks.

8 Conclusion
- Animals have rights. We should respect them.

Stage 3: Drafting your speech

Before Nazrul drafted his speech, his teacher reminded him what they had learned about the tricks of the trade from studying Matt's speech (see pages 32–33). Then Nazrul used his flow-chart to help draft his speech in paragraphs. Each of the eight points became a paragraph of writing.

When he had finished his first draft, Nazrul showed it to his teacher. His teacher thought his paragraph about zoos (below) was particularly good, because Nazrul had included questions which addressed the audience, and an example drawn from his own experience.

When you go to the zoo, do you ever think what it's like for the animals? How would you like to be shut up in a cage all the time? I remember this tiger we once saw in a zoo. It was pacing up and down its cage as if it was anxious about something. I kept thinking that it should have been roaming the forest instead of being penned in a cage.

But his teacher thought that Nazrul's opening (below) wasn't as good as it could have been.

I think the way we treat animals is cruel. There are lots of different types of cruelty to animals. In my speech I'm going to tell you all about the different type of cruelty.

He suggested that Nazrul should try to redraft his opening to make it grab the audience's attention more. Below is Nazrul's redrafted opening.

People say the British are a nation of animal lovers. But we're not. We often treat animals cruelly. We lock up rabbits in cages, let dogs chase after foxes and test chemicals on mice. The way we treat animals is a disgrace.

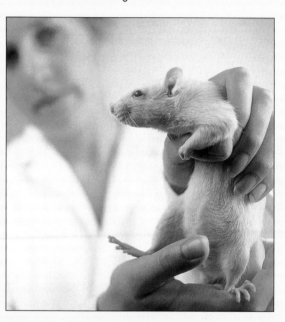

Notice that Nazrul has not only made it a much more powerful opening, he's even included a list of three!

Writing

Research, plan and draft a speech of your own. You could prepare a speech about animal rights issues or about environmental issues, such as pollution and waste, and what we need to do about them. Or you could choose some other subject that you care about.

Delivering Your Speech

The impact your speech has on your audience will depend not only on its content, but on how you deliver your speech.

Here are some things you need to think about when you are making a speech.

1 **Eye-contact.** Make sure you look at the audience every now and then. It helps to keep their attention. Don't spend all the time looking down at your script.

2 **Tone.** You can show how strongly you feel about something by varying the tone of your voice. If you do not vary the tone of your voice, your audience may get bored.

3 **Volume.** Speak loudly enough to be heard at the back of the room, but do not shout. Make sure you speak clearly and don't mumble. If you raise your voice at important parts in your speech, it helps to make them sound important.

4 **Pace.** Speak at a normal pace. If you speak too slowly, your audience may 'switch off'. If you speak too fast, they will not be able to understand what you are saying. Try not to say 'um' or 'er' and to make unnecessary pauses.

5 **Body language.** Stand up straight and try to look confident, even if you are feeling very nervous. Now and again use hand gestures to help to make a particular point, but don't overdo it. If you make too many gestures, it can be distracting.

Speaking and Listening

- On your own, study the advice on how to deliver your speech. List what you consider to be the five most important pieces of advice. Then form groups and compare your lists.
- Take it in turns to deliver your speech. At the end of each speech, give the speaker marks out of ten for the delivery of their speech. Discuss which things they did well and which things they could improve.

If you make too many gestures, it can be distracting.

Animal Experiments – A Debate

A **debate** is a formal discussion in which opposing views are expressed. People speak for and against a viewpoint which is called a **motion**. The motion is always presented in a formal way, which begins: 'This house believes that ...'

Speaking and Listening

Organise a class debate on the motion 'This house believes that animal experiments are necessary and it would be wrong to ban them.'

- Start by splitting the class into groups. Decide which groups are going to prepare speeches *for* the motion and which groups are going to prepare speeches *against* the motion. Then study the information on these two pages, and in your groups discuss the arguments you are going to use in your speeches.

- Next, choose four people to be the main speakers – two to speak for the motion and two against it. In your groups, help these people to prepare their speeches.

- Hold the debate and vote on the motion.

Testing Times – Animal Experiments

Each year, millions of live animals are used in laboratory experiments:
- to develop and test new medicines and vaccines (for both humans and animals);
- in scientific research into the workings of human and animal bodies and the diseases which affect them;
- to test the safety of new cosmetics, household cleaners and industrial and agricultural chemicals (for example, pesticides).

Much of this testing is required by law, in an effort to safeguard human health and the environment.

Animals used range from mice and rats bred specially for the laboratory, to endangered species taken from the wild, such as chimps, to pets stolen from their owners.
Mice (54.5%)
Rats (25%)
Rabbits and guinea pigs (10%)
Others* (10%)
Dogs and cats (0.5%)
*Others = chimps, macaque monkeys, armadillos, pigs, sheep and horses.

Animal Testing – Some Questions and Answers

Q: Are the tests controlled by law?

A: Yes – In Britain, they're regulated by the Animals (Scientific Procedures) Act 1986. Laboratories must be licensed by the Home Office and open to official inspection.

Q: Which are the main tests involved?

A: ● The Draize test – testing products on rabbits to see if they irritate eyes or skin. The substance, for example shampoo, is dripped into the rabbit's eyes.

● Skin sensitivity test – the product is applied to the shaved skin of a rabbit or guinea-pig to see if it has any side-effects, such as soreness or redness.

● Toxicity (poisoning) test – the substance is added to food or water and force-fed to mice or rats to test how poisonous it is. This is also known as the LD50 test (Lethal Dose 50%) because a product is tested to see how much of it can be taken before half of the sample of animals used dies.

Q: Do the tests cause suffering?

A: Yes, inevitably, although British labs have modified tests in recent years to reduce the suffering involved. Many tests are carried out without any anaesthetic or pain relief (though not all need them). Although anaesthetic is required by law, a special certificate can be granted if an experiment will not work with an anaesthetised animal.

Q: Don't people object to this?

A: Yes, they do. Opinion polls conducted by the RSPCA show that 95% of people are opposed to animal testing of household products and 96% to testing of cosmetics. More and more people are turning to products marked 'cruelty-free' or 'not tested on animals'. For many people, though, medical testing is a trickier matter.

Is Medical Testing Valid?

Many people agree, to an extent at least, with the use of animals in medical experiments. In their opinion, the testing of new drugs for the treatment of life-threatening diseases, such as AIDS and cancer, can be justified as essential research for the advancement of human health and science in general. Many diseases, such as polio, tuberculosis and smallpox, would still be fatal without the advances made through animal experimentation. In fact, smallpox has now been completely eradicated.

Doctors might argue that if we can prevent human suffering through scientific knowledge, we should do it. But is research always accurate – and are experiments always necessary? Many animals do not provide good models for humans and some drugs which are lethal to them, such as Aspirin and Penicillin, are vital to us, while some which cause no reaction in animals have caused side-effects in humans. And diseases like lung cancer could, in many cases, be prevented just as well by avoiding cigarettes.

Writing

Write a letter to a newspaper expressing your views on using animals for experiments. Make sure you use the proper layout for a formal letter (see page 16).

A Scottish Ballad

A **ballad** is a type of poem that tells a story. It usually consists of a number of short verses with a strong beat or rhythm to keep the story moving at a fast pace.

The first ballads were spoken or sung rather than written down. They told stories of love and heroism, mystery and adventure. Many ballads contain some dramatic dialogue and they sometimes have a chorus at the end of each verse, which the audience can join in and chant.

Reading

'Sir Patrick Spens' (page 41) is a Scottish ballad which tells the story of a Scottish tragedy. It uses a Scottish dialect (the language spoken in a particular part of Scotland), and because it is so old it includes a number of words that are not very common today. For example, the word 'ere' is used rather than the modern word 'before'.

Work in pairs and use the glossary which is printed beneath the poem to help you to read and understand the poem. (The glossed words are marked with an asterisk.)

Speaking and Listening

- In groups, discuss the story that is told in the ballad. Use these questions to help you.

1 What does the King want someone to do?
2 Why does he choose Sir Patrick Spens?
3 How does Sir Patrick Spens react when he gets the King's letter?
4 How do his crew feel about the voyage?
5 What happened to the ship and its crew?

- Now take it in turns to retell the story to each other. Use your own words and do not worry if you miss out or change some of the details, so long as you include the most important parts of the story.

- Prepare and act out a reading of the poem. Work in a group of five, with two people acting as storytellers, and the three others taking the parts of the King, Sir Patrick Spens and the crew member. You could tape-record your reading and add music and sound effects to help to make it more dramatic.

Sir Patrick Spens

The King sits in Dunfermline town
   Drinking the blood-red wine:
'O where will I get a skilly* skipper
   Will sail this good ship of mine?'

Then up and spake* an eldern* knight
   Sat at the King's right knee:
'Sir Patrick Spens is the best sailor
   That ever sailed the sea.'

The King has written a braid* letter
   And sealed it with his hand,
And sent it to Sir Patrick Spens
   Was walking on the strand.*

The first word that Sir Patrick read,
   A loud laugh laughed he;
The next word that Sir Patrick read,
   The tears blinded his e'e.

'O who is it has done this deed,
   And told the King of me,
To send me out at this time of year
   To sail upon the sea?

'To Noroway,* to Noroway,
   To Noroway o'er the foam.
The King's daughter of Noroway
   'Tis I must bring her home.

'Make haste, make haste, my merry
   men all,
   Our good ship sails the morn.'*
'O say not so, my master dear,
   For I fear a deadly storm.

'I saw the new moon late yestere'en*
   With the old moon in her arm;
And if we go to sea, master,
   I fear we'll come to harm.'

They had not sailed a league,* a league,
   A league but barely three,
When the sky grew dark, the wind
   blew loud,
     And gurly* grew the sea.

The anchor broke, the topmast lap,*
   'Twas such a deadly storm.
The waves came o'er the broken ship
   Till all her sides were torn.

O lang,* lang may their ladies sit
   With their fans into their hand,
Or ere* they see Sir Patrick Spens
   Come sailing to the land.

O lang, lang may the ladies stand
   With their gold combs in their hair,
All waiting for their own dear lords
   That they shall not see mair.*

And many was the feather bed
   That floated on the foam,
And many was the good lord's son
   That never mair came home.

Half o'er, half o'er to Aberdour,*
   'Tis fifty fathom* deep,
And there lies good Sir Patrick Spens
   With the Scots lords at his feet.

Anonymous

skilly skilful	**Noroway** Norway	**league** a distance of	**ere** before
spake spoke	**the morn** in the	about 3 miles	**mair** any more
eldern elderly	morning	**gurly** very rough	**Aberdour** a Scottish town on the
braid long	**yestere'en** yesterday	**lap** split	North Sea coast
strand shore	evening	**lang** long	**fathom** about 6 feet (1.8 metres)

A Modern Ballad

The Ballad of Homeless Jack

You'll pass him in the doorway,
you'll see him in the street,
with a blanket on his shoulders,
second-hand shoes on his feet.

You'll hear him squeeze from his whistle
a tune that's cracked and strange.
You'll see his hat left hopefully
to gather up your change.

Nobody stops to speak to him,
nobody catches his eye,
from the stream of hurrying people
who pass so swiftly by.

With a grubby bundle in his hand
and a charity coat on his back,
you'll meet him all across the land.
His name is Homeless Jack.

Now some say Jack is lazy,
and some say Jack is bad,
and some say Jack's a hopeless case,
a junkie, drunkard, mad.

But Jack says he's a human being,
not far from me or you.
He sees no point, he has no hope,
so what is Jack to do,

but sit upon his blanket
and let the world walk on
till life at last deserts him
and even dreams are gone?

And maybe as we hurry by
and look the other way,
we know that in the doorway
it could be us one day.

So why not spare for Homeless Jack
a coin, a nod, a grin,
to hold the tide of hopelessness
from coldly creeping in?

Tony Mitton

In Groups

Discuss these questions. Make notes of your answers. Then choose a spokesperson to share your ideas in a class discussion.

- Who is 'Homeless Jack'? Study the first four verses. What details does the poet give of: **a** his appearance; **b** his life; **c** the way people treat him?

- Discuss verses 5, 6 and 7. What does the poet say in them about: **a** people's attitudes towards Homeless Jack; **b** Homeless Jack's thoughts and feelings about life?

- Discuss the last two verses. What do they ask people: **a** to think about whenever they pass Homeless Jack; **b** to do when they see him? What is the message of these verses?

Writing and Performing

Imagine you have been asked to produce a performance of 'The Ballad of Homeless Jack' on television. Choose three verses and make a storyboard showing how you would present them.

Before you begin, study the ideas that Stephanie and Nadya produced for verse 1 (below). Notice how they include details not only of the scene and what happens, but of the type of camera shots they want. They also say how the lines should be spoken and include details of any music or sound effects they would use. (Like Stephanie and Nadya, you may need more than one frame for each verse.)

Note: The pictures in your storyboard only need to be sketches. What matters is your ideas!

Share your storyboard ideas in a class discussion. Then, as a class, work together and develop a performance of the whole poem. Rehearse it, then make a video-recording of your performance to show to another class in your year.

You'll pass him in the doorway,
you'll see him in the street,
with a blanket on his shoulders,
second-hand shoes on his feet.

Verse 1, Frame 1. This takes place in the half-light of evening. Low, mournful music is playing. People are hurrying home from work along a busy pavement. The camera races along with the people, who ignore the shapes of the homeless huddled in shop doorways.

Verse 1, Frame 2. The music gets louder as the camera gradually slows down until it picks out one of the homeless people. He has a blanket on his shoulders and shoes that are falling apart. Then the music stops and a single voice speaks the first four lines.

Reading

Use the library to find copies of other ballads and share them with the rest of the class. You could make a class 'Book of Ballads' by photocopying them and putting them in a folder. Each find a ballad to include in the book and write a short introduction saying what the ballad is about and why you chose it. Then staple your introduction to the photocopy of the ballad and put it in the folder.

Writing Your Own Ballads

Follow these guidelines to plan and write your own ballad.

1 Choose a suitable story

A ballad tells a story, so the first thing you need to do is to choose the story you are going to tell. Work with a partner and discuss possible ideas for ballads. Here are some ideas for the type of story that you could turn into a ballad:

- A sensational news story – for example, an accident such as a road, rail or air crash or an oil spill at sea; a fire or an explosion; a dramatic rescue.

- A story about a famous sporting hero and their achievements – for example, the achievements of a world champion such as the boxer Prince Naseem Hamed or the racing driver Damon Hill.

- A local ghost story or urban myth – for example, the story of the driver who picks up a hitch-hiker that turns out to be the ghost of someone killed in an accident.

- A tragic love story – for example, a story you make up about someone whose partner is either killed in an accident or dies from a fatal illness shortly after they have married.

- A cautionary tale – for example, the story of a teenager who takes drugs or gets involved in crime.

2 Research the story

- If your ballad is based on a true story, you will need to find out important details such as the date when it happened, the names of the people involved and of the place where it occurred. Use books, newspapers and CD-ROMs to research your story and make notes of all the important details.

- If your ballad is based on a story that you are making up, you will need to make up details, such as the names of people and places and the dates and times of key events.

3 List the main events

Make a list of the main events in the story. This will give you an idea of how many verses you will need to have.

4 Choose a verse form

- Many ballads have verses of four lines each. In 'Sir Patrick Spens' (page 41), line 2 in each verse rhymes with line 4. In other ballads, lines 1 and 2 of each verse rhyme and lines 3 and 4 rhyme.

- The lines in each verse of ballads have a regular rhythm. 'In Homeless Jack' (page 42), the verses have a beat pattern of 4 3 4 3 (that is, lines 1 and 3 of each verse have four beats, while lines 2 and 4 have three beats). In other ballads the beat is sometimes 4 4 4 4.

5 Draft the first verse

One way of beginning your ballad is to say where and when the events happened. Below is how Emma began her ballad about the oil tanker, the *Sea Empress*, which ran aground off the Welsh coast, spilling thousands of tonnes of oil.

> In February ninety-six,
> 'Sea Empress' came to port.
> It should have been an easy task,
> Or so the sailors thought.

Another way of starting is to say in your first verse who or what the ballad is going to be about. Below is how Farhan began his poem, 'The Ballad of Prince Naseem'.

> This is the tale of Prince Naseem
> And all the fights he's won;
> Of how he boxed his way to fame,
> To be the champion.

6 Draft the ballad

As you draft your ballad, make sure you keep to the rhythm and the rhyme-scheme of the verse form that you are using.

- If you are having trouble with the rhythm of the lines, count the syllables to make sure that you have the right number of syllables in each line. Try clapping out the rhythm and reading the verses aloud to a friend.

- If you are having trouble thinking of a rhyme for a particular word, ask your friends for suggestions or look for words that rhyme with it in a rhyming dictionary, such as *The Penguin Rhyming Dictionary*. Whatever you do, avoid including a word just because it rhymes.

7 Publish your ballad

Publish your ballad by making a neat copy of it on a word processor. Make sure you read it carefully to check the spelling and punctuation, before printing it out. You could then illustrate it, mount it and make a wall display of your ballads.

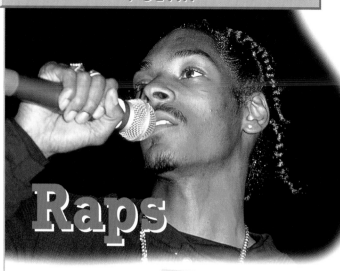

Raps

Raps, or rap poems, have a strong rhythmic beat and are often spoken to music. They are written to be spoken and performed. Because of this, the language of rap poems contains the type of words and phrases that are common in speech.

Many rap poems are written in a dialect. Raps often include words, expressions and grammatical forms that are found in Caribbean dialects.

The poem on this page is a rap that also tells you how to write a rap.

WRITE-A-RAP RAP

Hey, everybody, let's write a rap.
First there's a rhythm you'll need to clap.
Keep that rhythm and stay in time,
'cause a rap needs a rhythm and a good strong rhyme.

The rhyme keeps coming in the very same place
so don't fall behind and try not to race.
The rhythm keeps the rap on a regular beat
and the rhyme helps to wrap your rap up neat.

'But what'll we write?' I hear you shout.
There ain't no rules for what a rap's about.
You can rap about a robber, you can rap about a king,
you can rap about a chewed up piece of string ....
(well, you can rap about almost .... anything!)

You can rap about the ceiling, you can rap about the floor,
you can rap about the window, write a rap on the door.
You can rap about things that are mean or pleasant
you can rap about wrapping up a Christmas present.

You can rap about a mystery hidden in a box,
you can rap about a pair of smelly old socks.
You can rap about something that's over and gone,
you can rap about something going on and on and on
and on ....

But when you think there just ain't nothing left to say ....
you can wrap it all up and put it away.
It's a rap. It's a rap. It's a rap rap rap rap RAP!

Tony Mitton

Speaking and Listening

In pairs, study Tony Mitton's poem about writing a rap (page 46).

- Discuss what he says about rhythm and how 'the rhythm keeps the rap on a regular beat'. One of you read the first two verses aloud, while the other claps out the rhythm, in order to see how the poem has a regular beat.

- What does the poem say about using rhyme? Which lines rhyme with which in his verses? What other rhyme schemes do you think you could use?

- What does the poem say about subjects you can write a rap about?

Writing

Work with a partner and draft a rap together. Do it in stages.

Stage 1: Choose a subject and do a brainstorm. A good way of getting ideas for a rap is to note down any words connected with your subject that rhyme.

Lawrence and Mihir decided to write a rap about football. Here are some of the rhymes they thought of.

score-draw-roar   grin-win
near-jeer-cheer
            boot-shoot
cup-up   crowd-loud   team-dream
    ball-wall   goal-soul

Stage 2: Think of how you are going to write about your subject. Lawrence and Mihir decided to write about someone dreaming about being the captain of the England football team.

Once they had thought of a way in to their subject, they began to draft their rap.

Stage 3: Draft your rap. Look at Lawrence and Mihir's first verse (below).

> Last night, man, I had this dream,
> Dreamed I was the captain of the England team.
> The manager, he says to me,
> 'Son, you gotta lead us to victory!'

Notice how they have managed to use a rap rhythm and have developed a verse in which lines 1 and 2 rhyme and lines 3 and 4 rhyme.

If you can't think of a way of getting started, use these two lines to begin your rap:

> Come on everybody, let's hear you clap,
> We're going to do the .... rap.

(Put in the name of whatever subject you are writing your rap about.)

Stage 4: Show your rap to another pair and ask them if they can suggest any ways of improving it. Then redraft your rap.

Stage 5: Prepare a performance of your rap. (You can find hints on how to perform a rap on page 49).

Raps to Read and Perform

In Pairs

Health Care

All yu Presidents
Think of de residents,
Queens an Kings
Start sharing,
City planners
Hav sum manners,
Prime ministers please
Think of de trees.

Those dat sail
Tek care of de whales,
De strong should seek
To strengthen de weak,
Lovers of art
Should play their part,
An all those upon it
Tek care of de planet.

Benjamin Zephaniah

Practise reading and performing this poem, then either make a tape-recording of your performance or present it to the rest of the class. Before you begin, read the advice on how to perform rap poems by Martin Glynn (below). Decide what mood you want your performance to create and try out different ways of dividing up the lines, before finally deciding which lines each of you is going to speak.

Before You Perform Your Rap ...

- Learn it! This doesn't mean you have to present it without a script. It just means that you have to have the confidence to use the script only as something to fall back on. Although most people who perform rap and dub poetry do learn it by heart, having the words with you on paper gives you confidence – and that's **crucial!** If you can learn your rap it will leave you free to do other things since you won't be holding pieces of paper. It can also be quite distracting to an audience to see bits of paper being waved about! If you perform as a small group, you could learn a bit each, then come together with a chorus line ...

- To learn it, either read it yourself a line at a time or record it on to a cassette player or video. Listen to it a number of times, until you start to remember it.

- Once you have learnt it, try **performing** it in several different ways until you find the one that you are happy with. Because it is a performance, you will find it never sounds the same twice, although some things, like the meaning, will remain the same.

- It is important to understand the **emotion** of your rap, so that you can convey this to an audience. It would be silly to write a poem about death, then read it in a funny voice (unless that is the effect you want to get over).

- Try your piece out on friends, who will give you constructive criticism to help build your confidence.

- After a few times performing to friends or family, you should be ready for a wider audience. As you grow in confidence you will find it easier to play and experiment with different styles.

- Go to it! Be a performer!

Speaking, Listening and Performing

Work with a partner. Discuss Martin Glynn's advice on how to perform rap poems (page 48), then each practise performing Yvonne Mitto's poem (below). Talk about the expressions and gestures you could use to put across Yvonne Mitto's message that it's tough being a teenager. Then, join up with another pair and each perform the poem. Discuss whose performance works best and why.

Teenage Meanage

Teenage
Meanage
What an age to be
I wanna be you
And you wanna be me
Fashions
Passions
Things you have to wear
Bright clothes
Right shoes
Then of course the hair
Can't be seen
To be coming off the scene
Might lose my cred
Mom sends me to bed

Teenage
Meanage
What an age to be
So much pressure
Coming from afar
Can't wait to come in late
Have my own car
Go to a bar
Stay out all night
Do things that aren't right
Have money
Jingling in my pocket
Sounds like honey
Teenage
Meanage
What an age to be

Yvonne Mitto

Describing Characters

When you watch a story on television, you can see what the characters are like from their appearance and how they speak and behave. It's different when you read a story. You have to build up a picture of the people in the story from what the author tells you about them.

Often writers introduce their characters by giving a pen portrait of them. A **pen portrait** is a paragraph that tells you some key information about a character. It usually tells you:

- a few facts about the person's appearance;
- something about what sort of person they are;
- something about the way the person behaves.

A good way of practising how to write a pen portrait is to write a pen portrait of someone you know, either a friend or a relative.

Below are John's pen portrait of his brother, Daniel, and Angela's pen portrait of her classmate, Leanne.

Daniel

He pretends to be grown up, although he isn't yet, and he's sarcastic and tries to make out he's bored with everything. He's quite tall, and not at all fat. His voice is breaking and that makes him angrier, because he thinks it sounds funny. He's got a bony sort of face and blue eyes.

Leanne

Leanne is quite small and pretty. She has long black hair and a dark face. In school she dresses in uniform. Outside school she wears denim jeans and a denim jacket. Her mother is from Mexico and her dad is from Jamaica, so she has an interesting face. She often wears thick red lipstick. She is lively and talkative and sometimes she gets into trouble for being rowdy in class.

Speaking and Listening

In pairs, study the pen portraits. Make notes about what you learn from them about the person's: **a** appearance, **b** character, **c** behaviour. Then form groups and compare your notes.

Writing

Write a pen portrait of one of your friends or relatives. Before you begin, make a list of the key facts that you are going to include in your description, then write your portrait of them.

Another way to describe a person's character is to pick out a key feature of their character and then to describe an incident which shows that feature of their character.

Often a description of a character doesn't just tell you about the person who is being described. It also tells you about the relationship between the person writing the description and the character they are describing. In the description of Steve Taylor below, by Brian Keaney, we learn about how much Danny dislikes Steve.

Steve

Steve Taylor is a thug. That is my word for him. When I first came to the school, I had the bad luck to get put in the same tutor group as him.

When Ms Bryant was calling the register on the first day, she paused at my name. 'Danny Dobretti?' she said. 'Have I pronounced that right?' Why she had to find it difficult I don't know. There are kids in my class with really weird names. But she had to pick on my name.

Steve Taylor was sitting on the other side of the class. He was already about six inches taller than everybody else. 'Did you say "Danny Dogbreath", Miss?' he called out.

Everyone laughed. Then Ms Bryant made things even worse by starting into a great long lecture about how you shouldn't make fun of other people's names. That really had a lot of effect. The first thing Steve Taylor did when the tutor period was over and we were filing out of the class, was slap me on the back and say, 'Hey, Dogbreath, lend us a pencil.'

Speaking and Listening

Read about Steve Taylor. In pairs, discuss what happens in the incident that is described and how it backs up Danny's statement that Steve Taylor is a thug.

Writing

Describe a person's character by writing an account of an incident in which they behave in a particular way. Either invent a character of your own or write about one of the following people:

- **Sally Rogers**, who is always getting into trouble for being cheeky;
- **Martin Major**, who is large and clumsy and gets bullied;
- **Nina Patel**, who is kind, caring and sympathetic;
- **Stephen Ashbourne**, who is sly and lets other people take the blame for things he does;
- **Jackie Slater**, who is very clever and is a goody-goody;
- **Thomas Thurston**, who is lazy and forgetful.

Using Dialogue

Writers develop the characters of the people in their stories by showing how they behave in the situations that occur in the story. You can tell what a person is like by what they say and do. So writers often use dialogue. How a person speaks and what they say helps to tell you what sort of person they are.

Here is part of a story by Maureen Duffy about four children who go trespassing. The children are a girl called Paddy, who is telling the story, and her three step-brothers – Fred (the eldest), Arthur and Billy (the youngest).

Scrumping

We set off through the park; past the mill, over the Minny Brook and out of the gates on the other side and then up the road. About a mile or so along we came to a disused camp, nissen huts with smashed windows that we peered through.

'I bet tramps come here and make fires,' said Arthur.

'Come on,' said Fred. 'I know a place.'

We followed him across fields to a road.

'Up here?' said Arthur.

'Yeah, there's walnut trees and apples. Scrumping,' answered Fred. 'Over that wall.' An impressive brick and wrought-iron gateway appeared in the wall and here there were foot and handholds.

'You keep look-out,' said Fred, 'and come up when I whistle.' He clambered up the wall and disappeared. Nothing moved on the damp road. There was a shrill whistle.

'Go on,' said Arthur to me.

'I want to go next,' Billy whined.

'She's going next. Go on.'

I began to clamber up the wall. It was no use saying no. At the top Fred reached down a hand and I hauled myself up flat on the top, heart thudding with fright.

'Jump,' said Fred.

'I can't.'

''Seasy.'

Slowly I lowered myself down the other side. Arthur came next and landed with a thump of heavy boots beside us. Billy was last, snivelling that we were going to leave him and he'd tell our mum.

Speaking and Listening

In groups, discuss these questions. Make notes of your answers, then share your views in a class discussion.

● What shows that Fred is the leader? List all the things that Fred says and does that show he is the leader.

● What do you learn about **a** Arthur, **b** Paddy, and **c** Billy from what they say and do?

● Imagine you were going to make a film of this incident. Discuss what sort of people you would be looking for to play the parts of the four children. Talk about what you think each of the children should look like and what clothes you think they should be wearing.

The story on pages 53–55 was written by Jenni Russell, when she was twelve.

Belfast Saturday

Jenni Russell

Seven o'clock.

Grey-haired Mrs Collins turned over in her bed, a huge mountain of flesh. The room was stuffy, but she could not open the window because the lock was broken, and there was no one to mend it since 'He' had died six years ago.

Her alarm-clock went off promptly at seven-five, and she slowly heaved her massive bulk out from underneath the bedclothes. She dressed herself slowly, shivering in the cold of the unheated room.

Miss Jeanie O'Flaherty had been up for an hour already. Tonight her boyfriend was taking her out, and she had been up early, pressing and ironing her best clothes.

Jeanie looked appraisingly at her reflection in the full-length mirror. She smiled suddenly at herself, then stood stock-still, listening, as she heard the faint rattle of gunfire.

'How far away?' she breathed to herself, hoping desperately, 'not here, Lord, not here, not again.' Last week she had seen a car pass and had watched, helpless, as two young teenage boys were mowed down with bullets. She was shaking now, re-living the terror of that moment, hearing the one boy's scream of agony, watching the other drop to the ground without uttering a sound.

Mrs Collins munched her cornflakes while she listened dispassionately to the news.

'... and these murders bring Ulster's civilian death toll to 637, since 1969. Now for the weather.'

She switched the radio off, and continued to eat. Mrs Collins had never been actively involved in the violence, and after the first shocks, when deaths were announced daily, she accepted everything with stoicism.

Fifteen minutes later, she was down on her knees, scrubbing the kitchen floor. Sean Collins has always liked a clean house. His photograph stood on top of the green wooden table in the corner of the room. She was glad that he had not lived to see 'these awful goings-on' as she termed it in her mind.

Breathing heavily, she pulled herself to her feet, took a duster, and polished, gently, the silver photograph frame. Sean Collins's face smiled up at her as she worked.

Carefully she replaced the photograph, and moved on to tidy her minute front-room.

There was nothing to tidy. She ran her duster quickly over the furniture, and sat down to rest in one of the uncomfortable armchairs. The last time any visitor had been in here, she recalled, was when the vicar came to tell her that Sean was dead.

Jeanie was washing up. Her next-door neighbour, Brigit Maloney, Jeanie's own age, was talking eagerly about make-up and dresses. Jeanie placed the last plate in the rack.

'Come upstairs, Brigit, I've laid out my clothes for this afternoon. Andrew's taking me out, you know.'

Brigit admired Jeanie's new dress, which was white-bordered with blue stripes. Jeanie was wearing it now, turning round and round slowly.

'Oh, won't you look lovely tonight!' Brigit breathed. 'Have you any blue eye-shadow? It would go with that ever so well!'

Jeanie shook her head. 'I couldn't afford it before, but I've been saving for three weeks and I'm going to buy it this afternoon.'

Ten minutes to two.

Mrs Collins, retired charwoman, grey-haired and humble, was out shopping at the nearby supermarket. She peered anxiously at Campbell's Soups, threepence off recommended price, or should she buy a packet soup, penny cheaper? She was pondering on the question, when she heard a shrill voice exclaiming:

'Look, Mum, that lady's dress is darned!'

Mrs Collins wished she could disappear. Pretending to be oblivious of the many faces turned in her direction, she continued staring at the soups, but she had never felt so flustered inside since, as a child, she had been made to stand on a stool in front of the school in disgrace.

Miss Jeanie O'Flaherty, shop assistant, off-duty, black-haired and strongly Catholic, looked sympathetically at the old woman, smoothing down her own blue dress while she did so. At three o'clock her boyfriend was coming to take her out, and Jeanie had bought a new dress for the occasion. Now she was running over the merits of different types of make-up in her mind. Only ten shillings to spend, and so many different kinds of lipstick, eye-shadow, cheek-shiner and nail varnish! Perhaps after all she had better buy that 'Glamor Girl' make-up box. It was so hard to decide – Jeanie glanced at the time. Five minutes to two.

Mrs Collins had decided on Campbell's Soups. After all, Sean had always preferred tinned soup when they could afford it, and besides, her grandchildren were coming to tea, little Mark, Barbara and Johnny. She thought affectionately of Barbara, nice little girl that she was, well-mannered and always polite – one of the reasons for visiting the supermarket was to buy a present for Barbara, whose birthday was in two days' time. Mrs Collins had saved for a month to be able to afford buying her granddaughter the eleven-shilling doll she wanted.

The old lady glanced down at her unpolished shoes, and wondered if she could afford just a tiny tin of shoe-polish. Mrs Collins found life hard these days, living on a minute pension while prices of goods grew higher and higher.

Jeanie stopped in front of a mirror and patted her hair into place. She looked unseeingly at the mirror, as her boyfriend told her that she was the most beautiful girl in the world. Then she was literally brought down to earth, as Mrs Collins walked into her. 'Sorry,' Mrs Collins said, and Jeanie was just scrambling to her feet, when –

Two o'clock.

The rescue workers dug for three hours before uncovering the bodies. Enough was left of Mrs Collins to be identified, but all that remained of Jeanie was a pile of ashes and a scrap of blue material fluttering forlornly in the wind –

Thinking About the Events

Read the story 'Belfast Saturday' through twice (pages 53–55), then write answers to these questions.

1 At what time does Mrs Collins get up?
2 What did Jeanie O'Flaherty get up early to do?
3 What did Jeanie O'Flaherty hear as she was admiring herself in the mirror?
4 What did Mrs Collins do after breakfast?
5 Who came round to see Jeanie after breakfast and what did they talk about?
6 Where were Jeanie and Mrs Collins at ten to two?
7 What things did Mrs Collins and Jeanie plan to buy?
8 At what time did Jeanie bump into Mrs Collins and what happened immediately afterwards?

Thinking About the Plot

In groups, discuss the ending of the story. Were you surprised? How does the writer introduce violence early on in the story? How is the tension built up?

Discuss the plot of the story. Talk about how the action is set at different times and how the writer switches from describing what one character is doing to describing what the other character is doing. Draw a diagram to show how the plot of the story develops and comes to its climax.

Thinking About the Characters

Study these statements about Mrs Collins and Jeanie O'Flaherty. Some of them are *true* and some of them are *false*. On your own, decide which ones are true and which are false, then form groups and compare your answers.

1 Mrs Collins is a widow.
2 Mrs Collins gets lots of visitors.
3 Mrs Collins is a Protestant.
4 Mrs Collins has plenty of money.
5 Jeanie is not worried by the violence.
6 Jeanie is a Catholic.
7 Jeanie has blond hair and blue eyes.
8 Jeanie has lots of money to spend on make-up.

In groups, talk about how the two characters are presented in the story. What do you learn about each of them from:

● the description of their appearance and clothes?
● the description of their background?
● what they do, think and say during the day?

Which of them are you able to picture most clearly? Whose lifestyle is more clearly described – Mrs Collins's or Jeanie O'Flaherty's?

Make notes of your ideas, then share them in a class discussion.

Role-play

Work in groups. One of you is a TV reporter, the others are either eye-witnesses or neighbours who knew Mrs Collins or Jeanie O'Flaherty. Develop a news report giving details of the explosion and containing interviews with eye-witnesses and people who knew Mrs Collins and Jeanie O'Flaherty.

Writing

Use 'Belfast Saturday' as a model to plan and write your own story about two people who meet each other because of an unexpected event. For example, they could each be involved in a road accident. Try to include lots of details about the two people, so that your readers will be able to picture them and their lifestyles.

Writing Your Own Story

Write your own story. Use the hints on these pages to help you to plan and draft your story.

Stage 1: Planning your story

Thinking about the plot

First, think about what is going to happen in your story. Most stories have a key event in them – a crisis point at which something dramatic happens. The characters in your story could find something out, be involved in an accident, get caught doing something they shouldn't have been doing, rescue a person or animal or have a narrow escape.

Think of dramatic events you have seen involving young people on TV programmes, films and videos. Could you use any similar event as the key event in your plot?

When you have chosen a key event for your story, write one or two sentences about the plot of your story. Here's what Nathan wrote about the plot of his story.

Plot

Carl has promised to look after Mrs Spencer's kitten. The kitten climbs up a ladder which is leaning against Mrs Spencer's bedroom window. Carl thinks the ladder belongs to Mr Knight, a window-cleaner. Carl tries to rescue the kitten by climbing up the ladder. The kitten goes through the half-open window. Carl climbs inside, sees the kitten – and two burglars.

Thinking about the characters

Decide who the main characters are going to be in your story. Give them names and ages and make brief notes about them – about their appearance, their character and their behaviour.

Here are the notes Nathan made about two of his characters.

Carl Downer

14 years old, tall and thin. Speaks fast, and bites his nails when frightened. Lives with his mum. Hasn't got many friends. Good with old people. Likes to hear their stories about the past.

Mrs Spencer

In her eighties. Lives alone, and rarely goes out. But stays with her sister once a year. A bit deaf, and her face is wrinkled. Hair thin and grey.

Thinking about the setting

Decide when and where the main events of your story are going to take place. Are they going to take place now, in the past or in the future? Where are they going to take place – in the town or in the country? Is there an important place, such as a classroom or a shop, a cave or a ruined house? If so, are you going to imagine such a place or are you going to base your description on a real place that you have seen?

When you have decided on the setting for your story, write a sentence or two about it. Here's what Nathan wrote about the setting for his story.

Setting

An old house with a large fenced garden, on the edge of a housing estate. All events take place in and around the house. (Like the house of my cousin Martin.)

Stage 2: Writing the first draft

Once you have thought about the plot, the characters and the setting for your story, you are ready to write the first draft. Before you begin, you will have to decide how you are going to tell the story.

Are you going to write as if you are one of the characters in the story, telling the story from their viewpoint? This is called writing a **first-person narrative**.

Gemma decided to write as if she was one of the characters in her story (below).

> I stood outside the hut waiting for Carla and Toni. If they didn't arrive soon, we would be late. I was beginning to feel unsure about the whole idea.

Or are you going to write as if you are someone describing the events from an outside viewpoint? This is called a **third-person narrative**.

Nathan decided to describe events from the outside, as if he was a storyteller who knew all about the events and the people involved (below).

> Carl Downer was looking forward to looking after Mrs Spencer's kitten. He liked its soft black fur and large green eyes. He also liked Mrs Spencer. She was friendly. She talked about the past, and sometimes she gave him home-baked cakes. He wanted to do her a favour, help her out.

Note: Although you have worked out a plan for your story, you do not have to stick to it. Sometimes the story does not seem to be working out well, or you get a much better idea as you are writing. If that happens, change your plan.

Stage 3: Redrafting your story

When you have completed the first draft of your story, discuss it with a partner. Use the questions below to help you suggest ways that your partner can improve their story by redrafting it.

- **Has the story got a good opening?** Does it grab the reader's attention? Can you suggest a different way of starting the story that would make the opening more dramatic?
- **Are the events of the story easy to follow?** Is there a point in the story where the reader needs to know more about what is going on?
- **Is there enough detail about the main characters?** Are you able to picture them clearly? Are you told enough about them to be able to understand what sort of people they are and how they behave?
- **Is the setting clearly described?** Can you picture it clearly? If you can't, what sort of extra details would help you to be able to picture it more clearly?

- **Has the story got a good ending?** Can you think of any other ways that the story could have ended? Would changing the ending of the story make it more effective?

Nathan showed his story to Jason. Jason told Nathan he thought it was really good, except for his description of the discovery of the burglars (below).

> Carl opened the window and climbed into the bedroom. He saw the kitten and two strange men putting Mrs Spencer's silverware into a sack. They were burglars. They turned, and at once they saw him. They tried to grab him, but he dived between the fat burglar's legs and ran for the stairs.

Jason suggested Nathan should include more detail in his description, and try to make it more exciting. On the top of page 59 is how Nathan redrafted this part of his story.

Carl carefully opened the window and slid inside the bedroom, falling onto Mrs Spencer's bed. He saw Curly asleep on the bed. However, he was not alone in the room. There were two strange men putting Mrs Spencer's silverware into sacks. They were obviously burglars. One was fat, the other thin. They turned when they heard Carl fall onto the bed. They noticed him at once.

Before the burglars could think, Carl leapt off the bed and dived between the fat man's legs. He ran for the stairs. He realised at once why there was a ladder outside Mrs Spencer's house. It did not belong to Mr Radcliffe, the window-cleaner, but to the two crooks.

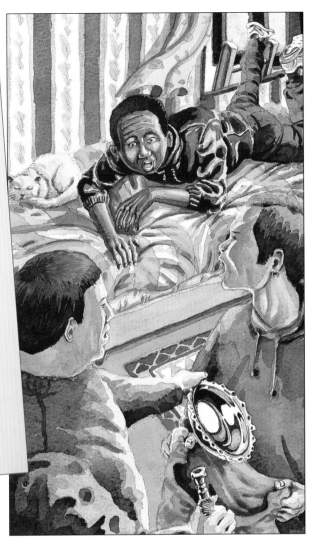

Stage 4: Checking spelling, grammar and punctuation

When you have redrafted your story, read it through carefully to check the grammar, spelling and punctuation. In particular, check your punctuation of any speech that you have included.

Stage 5: The final copy

Produce a final copy of your story. If you have been working on a word processor, you can print out enough copies of your story for everyone in the class to have a copy. You could get someone to design a cover, then bind your stories together and produce a class book of short stories.

In this unit you will be learning the story of William Shakespeare's play *Macbeth*. You will also be learning about how the English language has changed in the 400 years since Shakespeare wrote his plays.

William Shakespeare and the Elizabethan theatre

William Shakespeare (1564–1616) was born and grew up in Stratford-upon-Avon, but then moved to London. He wrote his plays during the reigns of Queen Elizabeth I (1558–1603) and King James I (1603–1625).

Shakespeare wrote thirty-seven plays. Some of his most famous plays are *Hamlet*, *Julius Caesar*, *Macbeth* and *Romeo and Juliet*.

These plays tell sad stories, which end in the death of the main character. A play that tells a tragic story, often ending in the death of the main character, is called a **tragedy**.

Some of his other plays tell stories that have happy endings. A play that tells a light-hearted story with a happy ending is called a **comedy**. Shakespeare's comedies include plays such as *Twelfth Night* and *A Midsummer Night's Dream*.

Many of Shakespeare's plays were performed at a theatre called the Globe. It was very different from a modern theatre. It had no roof, because there was no electricity in Shakespeare's time. So plays had to be performed in the open air, while it was still daylight.

Most of the audience stood in a yard in front of the stage and looked up at the actors. The entrance fee was one penny, which was a lot of money in those days. There were seats around the sides of the stage, but these cost two pence. Only the rich could afford to have seats.

The audience ate, drank and talked before the play began. During the performance, they ate nuts – rather like we eat popcorn at the cinema today. Going to see a Shakespeare play in those days was like going to see a blockbuster movie today. Shakespeare and his actors became rich and famous.

Speaking and Listening

In pairs, read and discuss what you learn from the passage (above) about Shakespeare and the Elizabethan theatre.

Research and Writing

Use books and CD-ROMs from the resources centre to find out more about Shakespeare and the Globe theatre. Then *either* draw a sketch of the theatre and write a paragraph describing it *or* imagine that you went to see a performance of a Shakespeare play at the Globe and write a diary entry about it.

Macbeth

Shakespeare's play *Macbeth* tells the story of what happens when a Scottish nobleman called Macbeth murders Duncan, the king of Scotland, so that he can become king himself. Pages 62–67 tell you the story of the play. This page introduces the main characters.

The Characters

Macbeth
He is an important nobleman – the Thane (Lord) of Glamis. Later he becomes King of Scotland.

Lady Macbeth
She persuades Macbeth to kill King Duncan. She becomes queen but her guilt drives her mad.

Duncan
King of Scotland
He is murdered by Macbeth.

Malcolm *and* Donalbain
Duncan's sons. They are blamed for Duncan's murder. Malcom goes to England and raises an army to fight Macbeth.

Banquo
An important nobleman, who is Macbeth's best friend. Macbeth hires some murderers to kill him and his son.

Fleance
Banquo's son. He manages to escape when the murderers try to kill him.

Macduff
An important nobleman. His wife and children are killed by murderers hired by Macbeth. He kills Macbeth.

Lady Macduff
and her son
They are murdered.

The Three Witches
They give Macbeth the idea that he can become king and that no one can beat him. They represent evil.

Macbeth and Banquo Meet the Three Witches

Macbeth and Banquo have just defeated a rebel army. They are on their way to see King Duncan.

They meet three witches.

The witches greet Macbeth, but ignore Banquo. They tell Macbeth that he will become king.

All hail Macbeth, Thane of Glamis.

All hail Macbeth, Thane of Cawdor.

All hail Macbeth – that shall be king hereafter.

Banquo asks the witches to give him a glimpse of the future. They tell him that he will never be king, but his children will be.

Lesser than Macbeth, and greater.

Not so happy, yet much happier.

Thou shalt get kings, though thou be none.

Macbeth wants to know how he will become king.

I am the Thane of Glamis, but the Thane of Cawdor is still alive! What you say is impossible!

But the witches disappear. Macbeth and Banquo are shocked.

They've melted – as a breath into the wind!

Have we gone mad?

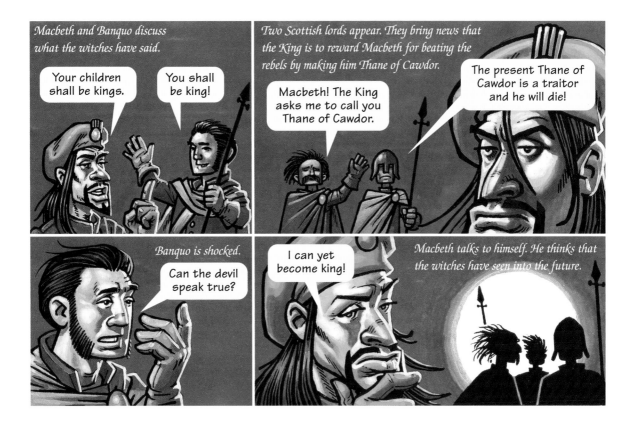

Reading and Writing

Read the picture-strip, then write answers to these questions.

1 Where were Macbeth and Banquo going and what had they been doing before they met the witches?

2 What did Macbeth find strange about the way the witches greeted him?

3 What did the witches say to Banquo?

4 What happened when Macbeth asked the witches to tell him more?

5 What important news do the two Scottish noblemen bring Macbeth?

6 What effect did the news have on: a Banquo, b Macbeth?

7 Imagine you are either Macbeth or Banquo. Write a diary entry describing what happened when you met the three witches and your thoughts and feelings about what they said.

Performing

● In groups, act out the scene in which Macbeth and Banquo meet the three witches. You can develop your own scripts and use your own words, so long as you do not miss out any key statements. If you are able to use either the stage or the drama studio you could experiment with lighting, music and sound effects to try to create atmosphere.

● Imagine that Banquo is telling the story of meeting the witches to his son Fleance. In pairs, take it in turns to be Banquo and Fleance. Before you begin, discuss the kind of questions that Fleance might want to ask Banquo. For example, what did the witches look like? How did they disappear?

Duncan is Murdered

Macbeth sends a letter to Lady Macbeth. He tells her what the witches said and how he has become Thane of Cawdor.

Hail, king that shall be!

Macbeth arrives home and Lady Macbeth persuades him to kill Duncan when he comes to visit them.

If you don't kill Duncan, you are a coward.

Duncan arrives at Macbeth's castle.

What a pleasant castle this is!

He shall not leave alive.

Macbeth sees an imaginary dagger. It is pointing him past the guards, who have been drugged, towards Duncan's room.

Is this a dagger which I see before me?

Macbeth tells Lady Macbeth he has killed Duncan. But he forgot to leave the daggers behind, so she takes them back and plants them on the guards.

I have done the deed.

Give them to me! I'll take them back!

Macduff finds Duncan's body. He raises the alarm.

O horror, horror, horror.

In the confusion that follows, Macbeth goes back and kills the guards

Duncan's sons are afraid they will be killed too, so they run away. Their flight is seen as a sign of guilt. They are blamed for Duncan's death.

I'll hide in England.

Speaking and Listening

Imagine you are a TV reporter sent to Macbeth's castle to report on Duncan's murder. Make notes of the key points you would want to include in your report, then take it in turns to give your reports to the rest of the class. (You could video record the reports and discuss whose was the best and why.)

Writing

● Imagine you are a Scottish lord appointed to investigate the circumstances of Duncan's death. Write the report that you would have written after you had questioned everybody about what happened.

● Work with a partner. Together produce a news-sheet reporting the news of Duncan's death. Before you begin, you may like to look at pages 72–74, which tell you how to write a news report. Draft your report on a word processor and, if possible, use a desktop publishing program to help you to design and print your news-sheet.

Banquo is Murdered

In Pairs

- Role-play a scene in which Fleance tells a friend about how he and Banquo were ambushed and how he feels about his father's death.
- Imagine you are two Scottish noblemen who attended the banquet. The following day you talk about Macbeth's behaviour at the banquet and the news you have heard of Banquo's death.

In Groups

Act out the scene at the banquet, when Macbeth talks to the murderers and then sees Banquo's ghost.

Writing

Write the entries for their secret diaries that **a** Macbeth, and **b** Lady Macbeth might have written that night after the banquet.

Macbeth Meets the Witches Again

Speaking and Listening

- In pairs, role-play the scene in which Macbeth tells Lady Macbeth what happened during his second visit to the witches.
- Imagine you are going to film this scene. Discuss your ideas for the setting and the kind of set you would want the designer to produce. Discuss how you would want the witches and the apparitions to look. What costumes would they wear? What make-up would they wear? What kind of background music would you play in order to create atmosphere?

Make notes of your ideas, then share them in a group discussion.

The Witches' Prophecies Come True

Speaking and Listening

In groups, discuss what happens at the end of the play.

- How does Lady Macbeth die?
- How does Macbeth die?
- How do the witches' prophecies come true?

- Who do you think was more to blame for what happened – Macbeth or Lady Macbeth?
- What do you think the message of the play is?

Make notes of your views, then choose someone to report them to the rest of the class and share your views in a class discussion.

Reading and Writing

Here are a number of statements about the events in *Macbeth*. Some of them are *true* and some of them are *false*. Work with a partner and decide which ones are true and which ones are false. Then form groups and compare your answers.

1 King Duncan rewarded Macbeth for putting down the rebels by making him Thane of Cawdor.

2 Duncan was murdered at Macduff's castle.

3 Lady Macbeth stabbed Duncan as he lay sleeping.

4 Macbeth gave orders for Banquo and his son Fleance to be murdered, but Fleance escaped.

5 The witches warned Macbeth to beware of Malcolm.

6 Lady Macbeth had such a guilty conscience that she started to sleepwalk.

7 The English army hid behind branches they had cut from Birnam Wood as they approached Macbeth's castle.

8 When Macbeth died, Fleance became king.

Speaking and Listening

In groups, imagine you are going to make a new film of *Macbeth*. Discuss the sort of people you think Macbeth and Lady Macbeth were.

● What were the main features of their characters?

● What do think they must have looked like?

● Which modern TV or film stars would you cast as Macbeth and Lady Macbeth?

Appoint someone to act as a spokesperson and share your ideas in a class discussion.

Writing

● Imagine you have been asked to write a book about Scottish kings. Write the chapter that you would write about Macbeth. Include all you know about him from Shakespeare's play, including details of the meetings he had with the witches.

● An **obituary** is a piece of writing about the life and achievements of someone who has just died. Write an obituary that might have appeared in a newspaper after Macbeth's death.

● An **epitaph** is a short piece of writing that is put on the gravestone of a person who has died. It may be in verse or prose. On the right is an example of an epitaph that Jack wrote for Banquo.

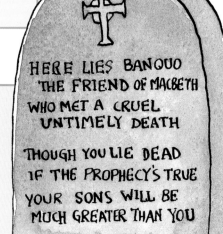

HERE LIES BANQUO
THE FRIEND OF MACBETH
WHO MET A CRUEL
UNTIMELY DEATH

THOUGH YOU LIE DEAD
IF THE PROPHECY'S TRUE
YOUR SONS WILL BE
MUCH GREATER THAN YOU

Write epitaphs to go on the tombs of:
a Duncan; **b** Banquo;
c Lady Macbeth; **d** Macbeth.

Shakespeare's Language

It is nearly 400 years since Shakespeare wrote *Macbeth*. The English language has changed a great deal during that time. Some words and expressions that Shakespeare used have dropped out of use. Other words have changed their meaning slightly, or their spelling has changed.

Below (left) is the letter which Lady Macbeth reads at the beginning of Act 1 scene 5. In it Macbeth tells her about his first meeting with the witches. On the right is a modern translation of it which Rhodri wrote.

They met me in the day of success; and I have learned by the perfect'st report they have more in them than mortal knowledge. When I burned in desire to question them further, they made themselves air, into which they vanished. Whiles I stood rapt in the wonder of it, came missives from the King, who all-hailed me 'Thane of Cawdor'; by which title, before, these weird sisters saluted me, and referred me to the coming on of time, with 'Hail, king that shalt be!' This have I thought good to deliver thee, my dearest partner of greatness, that thou mightst not lose the dues of rejoicing by being ignorant of what greatness is promised thee. Lay it to thy heart, and farewell.

The witches met me after we'd beaten the enemy. I have learned from reliable information that the witches are supernatural. I really wanted to question them further, but they disappeared into thin air. While I was still in a state of shock because of what had just happened, messengers from the King arrived and called me 'Thane of Cawdor'. This was just what the witches had called me. They also called me 'Future King.' I thought I ought to tell you this so that you wouldn't miss the chance of being able to rejoice at the thought that one day you're going to be queen. But keep it to yourself. Goodbye.

Reading and Writing

In groups, read the speech on the right and together work out a modern translation of it. Then compare your versions of the speech in a class discussion.

This speech comes from later in Act 1 scene 5. Lady Macbeth is persuading Macbeth that he must seize the opportunity to kill Duncan, while he is staying in their castle.

Lady Macbeth   O, never
Shall sun that morrow see!
Your face, my thane, is as a book where men
May read strange matters. To beguile the time,
Look like the time; bear welcome in your eye,
Your hand, your tongue; look like th' innocent flower,
But be the serpent under't. He that's coming
Must be provided for; and you shall put
This night's great business into my dispatch;
Which shall to all our nights and days to come
Give solely sovereign sway and masterdom.

In this unit you will be learning about how to write reports, articles and editorials for newspapers. You will also be writing, editing and publishing your own newspaper.

Planning Your Newspaper

There are two main decisions you must make when planning your newspaper. First, you must think about *who is going to read your newspaper*. For example, is your newspaper going to be aimed mainly at teenagers like yourselves? Or do you want it to have a wider readership? Is it going to be a newspaper aimed at everyone connected with the school, or everyone who lives in your neighbourhood?

Secondly, you must think about *what kind of newspaper it will be*. You must decide what its contents are going to be. Will it contain reports and articles about world events and issues? Or will it concentrate only on local issues or school issues?

Here are statements that two groups wrote once they had decided who they wanted to read their newspaper and what type of paper they were going to produce.

The Teenage Times

The Teenage Times is a newspaper that keeps you up-to-date with the things that matter to teenagers in the world today. There are up-to-date news items on all kinds of important world issues, such as pollution and the environment, and articles on topics such as careers and how to spend your leisure time. Written by teenagers for teenagers, the Teenage Times will keep you well-informed by giving you the facts you need to know about the world you live in.

The School Star

Keep up-to-date with what's really happening at school by reading The Star. We've the latest news on this year's charity walk, a behind-the-scenes look at rehearsals for the end-of-term musical and an interview with the caretaker. We've advice on how to get your homework done and still have time to go out. And how about this week's prize competition – win a free place on the day trip to France! Stay cool in school – read The Star!

Speaking and Listening

- In groups, discuss each statement. What does it tell you about **a** the readers the paper is aimed at; **b** its contents and the type of paper it is?

- Which paper do you think would be more interesting to read – *The Teenage Times* or *The School Star*? Give your reasons.

- Talk about the type of newspaper that you would like to produce and who you want to read it. Then discuss some possible names for your newspaper.

Writing

Draft a statement about your paper similar to those that the groups produced for *The Teenage Times* and *The School Star*.

Deciding on the Contents

Tara and her group decided to produce a newspaper like *The School Star* which focused on events and issues in their own school. They wanted it to appeal to everyone connected with the school, so they carried out some market research to find out the type of reports and articles people would want the newspaper to contain. They interviewed people and recorded their comments.

In groups, discuss what types of reports and articles *you* would like to see in a school newspaper. Make a list of the contents you would put in a school newspaper. Then share your ideas in a class discussion.

Questionnaires

Carry out some market research to find out what type of reports and articles people would like to read in the newspaper you plan to produce. You could survey people's opinions by drawing up a questionnaire and either writing down or tape-recording people's replies.

A **questionnaire** is a list of questions which can be used to find out people's views. There are two types of questions you can ask:

1 *Closed questions*. The answers people can give are limited to one of a list of choices. For example:

Do you think there should be a page of students' stories and poems?

Yes ☐   No ☐

The advantage of closed questions is that they provide information that is easy to analyse.

2 *Open-ended questions.* No choices are given, so people are free to answer in whatever way they like. For example:

What topics do you think there should be articles about?

The advantage of open-ended questions is that people are not forced to choose between your alternatives, but can choose how they answer, so you get a clearer idea of what their views are.

Draw up a questionnaire of your own. First look at the start of the questionnaire that Tara and her group drew up (below).

1 Who should we aim the paper at?
  (a) students only ☐
  (b) students and teachers ☐
  (c) students, teachers and parents ☐
  (d) everyone connected with the school ☐

2 What school issues would you like to read articles about?

_____

_____

_____

_____

3 Should there be articles about the school as it was in the past?

Yes ☐   No ☐

Newspaper Reports

Reading and Writing

Newspaper reports are written to a set pattern. They always contain information that answers a series of questions:
What? Who? Where? When? Why?

Study these two reports and write down how each of them answers these questions:

1 *What* happened?
2 *Who* was involved?
3 *Where* did it happen?
4 *When* did it happen?
5 *Why* did it happen?

The first two questions for the *Westward Gazette* article have been done for you.

1 What happened?
   A large black cat was found dead on a beach.

2 Who was involved?
   Bill Trewallis, a local fisherman.

Dead Beast Found in Cornish Cove

A large black cat was washed ashore on a remote beach in North Cornwall yesterday afternoon. It was found by a local fisherman, Bill Trewallis, aged 58. The creature looked as though it had been dead for some time.

A week before Bill had seen a large black creature on the cliffs near his cottage. 'It may have stumbled and fallen over the edge in the mist,' he said. 'It looked as though its neck was broken. But it had been in the water some time. It may have drowned.' The animal's body is to be examined by scientists to find out what it was and how it died.

Westward Gazette, 30 February 1998

Now then Sir, why are you driving this old croc?

By BILL MOULAND

Two Welsh policemen had the shock of their lives yesterday as 72-year-old Eugene Granat, a zoologist, was driving his African crocodile Scipio to the vet in Haverfordwest for an operation. Confused by the one-way system in the West Wales town, and worried about his fiery-tempered passenger in a cage on the back seat, Granat found himself going the wrong way up a steep hill.

As he tried to turn around, one of the car's wheels slipped from the edge of the pavement, leaving the vehicle dangling over a 4ft embankment. Summoned to the scene, PCs Declan Bulger and Stephen Cluett were only too glad to help – until they opened the door and saw Scipio's toothy grimace.

Knowing that they had to make a snap decision, the two constables drew lots – and it fell to PC Cluett to help Mr Granat lift the cage out of the car and into a police van.

Sergeant Kevin Jones of the Dyfed and Powys Constabulary said: 'The constables were a bit surprised. But I think the crocodile was more frightened of them than they were of it.'

Daily Mail, 7 February 1998

Reporting Styles

The same story is often reported differently in different newspapers. Each newspaper has its own reporting style. Here are two reports of the same story from different newspapers.

Jewellery Girl Suspended

A fourteen-year-old girl has been suspended from her school because she wore five ear-rings in each ear.

Her headteacher, Gerald Warren, said that teenager Amanda Stewart had been given a choice. She could either take the ear-rings out or go home.

Amanda's mother claims that her daughter did not want the holes in her ears to grow over. The rules at St George's Comprehensive School, Corbarton allow one stud in each ear only.

The Globe

OUT BY THE EAR!

Teenager Mandy Stewart has been thrown out of school and her ears are ringing.

Rebel Mandy got an earful when she turned up at St George's School, Corbarton with five rings in each ear.

It was too much for headteacher Gerald Warren, who ordered her to take them out. 'Our rules on jewellery are quite clear. It's up to her to obey them,' he said. When Mandy refused, he gave her a flea in her ear and sent her packing!

Mandy's mum, a hairdresser, was fuming with rage. 'It's ridiculous. It cost her a lot of money to get her ears pierced.'

The Gazette

Speaking and Listening

1 In groups, study the two reports and discuss the differences between them.

● Talk about the way the reports are written and the language that is used in them.

● Discuss the different headlines used.

● Which of the reports do you think is more interesting to read? Explain why.

2 Now think about your own newspapers. Which reporting style do you think would suit your newspaper – *The Globe's*, *The Gazette's* or some other style? Decide which style you are going to use.

Writing

Read the facts below and then write a newspaper report for your newspaper in the style of either *The Globe* or *The Gazette*.

★ NEWS FLASH ★ NEWS FLASH ★ NEWS FLASH ★

First prize in national songwriting competition won by local schoolgirl – Sophie Jenkins (14). Song 'It's Tough Being a Teenager' was written at school – Morgan High School, Davidstown. Competition was organised by 'TV Talentspotters'. Sophie was invited to sing on the show in January 1999. Sophie's brother Euan plays the drums in the successful pop group Scream.

Interviewing for News Reports

Many news reports are based on interviews with people. The reporter asks questions to find the answers to the five key questions – *What? Who? Where? When? Why?* Often they will also ask: *How did it happen?*

Among the news stories that you could put in your newspaper are reports of incidents that have happened to you and your friends.

Speaking, Listening and Writing

In pairs, take it in turns to interview each other about an important event in your life, such as when you achieved something special or were involved in a dramatic event like a rescue or an accident.

Write down the answers to your questions, so that you can use the information as the basis for a newspaper report. Make sure you are accurate with the facts. For example, check that you spell the names of people and places correctly.

Before you begin, study the interview below in which Carleen asked Curtis about the time when he fell off his skateboard and was taken to hospital.

Q. What is your name?

A. Curtis Freeman.

Q. Where do you live?

A. 44 Arncroft Road, Northbury.

Q. How old were you when the accident happened?

A. Thirteen.

Q. When did it occur?

A. On the morning of Saturday 14 June – a week after my birthday.

Q. What exactly happened?

A. I was practising on my skateboard on the tarmacked area in Priestlands Park when this labrador dog ran straight in front of me. I fell off and landed awkwardly on my left arm.

Q. What did you do?

A. I went to the casualty department at Queen's Hospital. They X-rayed my arm and found it was broken, so they put it in plaster.

Q. Have you had any other accidents on your skateboard?

A. No. My mum contacted the council and now they've put a fence round, so that dogs can't get into the skateboarding area.

Writing

- Use the information that Carleen collected from her interview with Curtis and write a report on Curtis's accident.

- Write a newspaper report based on the information you got from interviewing your partner. Plan your report so that the most important information goes in the first paragraph. Try to include at least one quotation and think of an interesting headline.

Editorials

A newspaper's **editorial** is an article that expresses an opinion on a particular topic in the news. It is written by the editor or another senior member of staff. The writer often refers briefly to the news story and produces arguments and evidence to back up their opinion.

Here is an example of an editorial written by students for their group's newspaper.

Don't Get Deafened!

Recent research suggests that just one night in an all-night disco can permanently damage your ears. It's time our generation woke up to the fact that we're in danger of deafening ourselves.

It's all very well saying that we like loud music and that's the way it's supposed to be. More and more young people are having to face the fact that they can no longer hear normal conversations.

The solution is simple. Start wearing earplugs. It may not seem the coolest thing to do, but it's certainly the wisest.

The choice is yours: either risk your friends taking the mickey or risk losing your hearing. I know which I'd prefer.

Speaking and Listening

In groups, discuss the opinion expressed in this editorial. What kind of language is used? What arguments are used to back up the opinions? Are they convincing? Give your reasons.

Writing

Write an editorial expressing your opinions about an issue that is currently in the news. Either choose your own topic or write your views about one of the following topics:

- wearing fur coats;
- restricting smoking in public places;
- how much pocket money teenagers should get;
- making roads safer for pedestrians and cyclists;
- banning all bloodsports.

Feature Articles

As well as news reports, newspapers contain feature articles on topics of particular interest to their readers. A **feature article** is an article in a newspaper or magazine that covers a topic in an extensive and interesting way.

The article on canoeing in this chapter is from a newspaper for young people.

PADDLE POWER!

Take one kayak, a paddle, then add water – welcome to the world of canoeing

Originally made from hollowed out tree trunks, canoes and kayaks have been used as transport for thousands of years. These days canoeing is one of the UK's most exciting sports – as long as you don't mind getting wet! It's great fun and a brilliant way to spend time outdoors. So whether you want to compete, play games or go on leisurely day trips, here's how to get paddling.

You don't need to be a brilliant swimmer, but if you feel a bit nervous it's best to learn the basic skills in an indoor pool. Start by joining a canoe club or go to an adventure centre.

Kayaks – canoes with closed tops – are mainly used for racing and adventure canoeing, while open canoes are good for family trips or beginners with special needs.

One of the first skills you must learn is how to capsize properly (don't worry, you will be wearing a buoyancy aid at all times). A kayak can overturn quite easily because of its shape, but once you've got the hang of rolling it

Still waters for beginners

It's white, it's wet and it's wild! Going white-water canoeing on one of Britain's bubbliest rivers

upright again, that's the scary bit over!

Next, you will be taught how to use the paddle. The basic strokes are forwards, backwards, draw-strokes (to move sideways), sweep-strokes (to turn round) and reverse strokes for emergency stops.

Once you've mastered the basic skills, you'll be ready to go out on a canal, river or lake. Often one 90-minute session in a pool will be enough to build your confidence.

The great thing about canoeing is that you can become good quite quickly – and then the fun really starts. Clubs organise all sorts of team games from canoe polo to

rafting. In rafting, all the canoes are pulled together like a large raft and you have to run between them – the trick is making sure you don't slip in!

Clubs can also arrange day trips. It's a great way of seeing wild animals and birds close-up – but you have to be very quiet!

For the more energetic, there's all kinds of canoe racing from white-water and slalom to sprint racing, which is an Olympic event.

For details of your nearest canoe centre and more information, write to: British Canoe Union, Adbolton Lane, West Bridgford, Nottingham NG2 5AS.

Reading and Writing

Read the article on canoeing and write answers to these questions.

1 Pick out the words and phrases used that make canoeing seem a thrilling activity **a** in the headline, **b** in the captions, and **c** in the first paragraph .

2 List the key facts about canoeing that you learn from this article.

3 Draw a flow-chart, showing how the article is arranged in paragraphs, each of which deals with a separate topic.

   Below is the start of such a flow-chart.

Paragraph 1
Introduction – What canoeing is. It's fun.

Paragraph 2
The best way to start.

Paragraph 3
The difference between kayaks and open canoes.

4 Pick out the paragraphs in which people's feelings are mentioned.

5 Say what you think about canoeing from having read the article. Is it an activity that you would like to try? Give reasons for your answer.

Writing

Write a feature article on any topic that you think readers of your group's newspaper would find interesting. For example, you could write about another activity, such as go-karting, disco-dancing or forming a band, about the latest fashions or about getting a part-time job.

Plan and draft your article carefully.

- Begin by making a list of at least five main points you want to make in your article.

- Plan your article in paragraphs. (You could draw a flow-chart showing what each paragraph is going to be about.)

- Try to think of an introduction that will capture your readers' attention.

- Write a first draft, then show it to a friend. Ask them which parts they found most interesting, and to suggest how you might change the parts that were the least interesting.

- Redraft your article and think up an eye-catching headline for it.

- Read your article again to check the grammar, spelling and punctuation.

- Use a word processor to produce the final copy of your article.

Editing and Publishing Your Newspaper

Now that you have learned how to write reports, articles and editorials, you can plan, write and publish your newspaper.

Speaking and Listening

In groups, hold an editorial meeting. Decide how many pages your newspaper is going to have and what the contents of each page are going to be.

You will have to think about what size your pages are going to be. Find out if there is a **DTP** (desk-top publishing) program available that you could use and, if possible, use a computer to design and print your newspaper.

Check what size pages the DTP program can produce. Then draw up a plan showing what is going to go on each page.

Finally, decide which members of the group are going to be responsible for each page. Each person should be responsible for one or two pages. They are going to edit those pages.

Editing Your Page

As editor of a page, it is your job to collect the reports and other items that are going on that page, to plan the layout of the page and to check the page before it is printed.

Planning the layout. You need to decide the number of columns you are going to have on your page and the distance between them. You can set this up on the screen in the form of a grid.

The layout you choose will depend on how many different items you want to fit onto your page. Beware of trying to fit too much in, otherwise your page will look cluttered. Remember to leave room for headlines.

Cutting a report. You may find that you cannot fit everything onto the page. If that happens, you may have either to leave out one of the items or to rewrite one of the reports to make it shorter.

Writing

Study the report (below) which is 175 words long.
Cut it and rewrite it so that it is only 80 words long.

Pop Star Visits School

Brit Pop singer Tina Taggart from the group 'Overexcited' visited our school, Papermill Comprehensive, Undercliffe, Loamshire, last week.

Tina Taggart, lead singer of 'Overexcited', was once a student at our school. Although Tina, a former student, did not do well in most subjects, she was a good musician and gained an A grade at GCSE. She did not do so well in English, maths, science or history. But she was good at sport.

Our headboy, Jamie Hurling, greeted the singer and she was taken to the headmaster's study. Mr Clarkson, our headmaster, gave the star a cup of coffee, and later he showed Tina the whole school.

The singer, Tina Taggart, has donated money for the school to build a sports dome. This will help us to build up our physical skills. At present all sport is done in the Main Hall, which is also used for assemblies.

Tina visited the music room. She and our music teacher, Mr Bruce, sang a few songs together. Tina left before lunch to finish recording her new album.

Checking Your Page

Before you print out your page, check it carefully.

- Check for spelling errors and mis-typings.
- Check that any graphics or pictures are in the right place and have the right captions.
- Check that headlines are in the right place and that you have left a space between them and the text of the report, so that they stand out.
- Check that the punctuation is correct and that each piece of writing is in proper paragraphs. There should be a line space between each paragraph.

- Check that you have always used capital letters correctly for names of people and places, and that 'I' is always a capital letter.
- Make sure that dates are presented correctly – 17 (space) May (space) 1999.
- Make sure that you have put a space after each punctuation mark.

When you have read your page carefully, get someone else to check it as well before you print it out.

Words and Pictures

Advertisers use a mixture of words and pictures to try to make places seem attractive and to persuade you to visit them. When they are advertising family holidays, they try to make out that there is lots to do and that everyone will have fun – no matter what age they are.

Speaking and Listening

In groups, study the advertisement for Butlin's Somerwest World (page 81).

- Discuss the choice of pictures. How do they suggest:
  a that a holiday at Somerwest World is fun;
  b that people of different ages will enjoy themselves;
  c that there is plenty to do there?

- Discuss the heading at the start of the description and how it is made to stand out **a** by printing it in capitals; **b** by the use of **alliteration** (using several words together that all begin with the same sound).

- Study the description. List what it tells you about the facilities, the activities and the entertainment at Somerwest World.

- Talk about the language used in the description. Pick out words and phrases that are used to suggest everyone will really enjoy themselves at Somerwest World.

- Study the sentence in the section 'Out & About'. List the adjectives that are used to make the places you can visit appear interesting.

- What else do you notice about the list of places in the 'Out & About' section? (Look at page 33 for a clue.)

Writing

Imagine that you visit Somerwest World and that you are asked to write a postcard describing what an enjoyable time you are having, so that it could go in their next brochure. Include lots of adjectives in your description in the way that an advertiser would.

Adjectives – A Reminder
Adjectives tell you more about a noun.
If it's <u>small</u> or <u>pretty</u>, <u>bright</u> or <u>brown</u>.

Somerwest World
Minehead, Somerset

A HOLIDAY WHERE EVERY DAY IS DIFFERENT

If you enjoy the kind of holiday where every day is different, you need look no further. For children especially, every hour can be different, with fabulous clubs and games, an all-weather multi-sports court, indoor sports arena and fun-filled activities such as ten pin bowling, so there's never a dull moment.

You could try out a new sport yourself and take the opportunity of being coached by professionals. There's also a gym to work out in, sauna and solarium to relax in, and, of course, our seafront funfair and exciting new waterworld.

No two evenings need be the same either. A quiet drink or meal followed by a memorable show, we'll make it an evening with a difference.

☎

TO BOOK CALL US NOW ON

0990 011 011

OR SEE YOUR TRAVEL AGENT

Disneyland Paris Resort Hotels

If you decide to stay in one of the Disneyland Paris Resort Hotels there is a superb selection to choose from. Offering good quality value for money are the Hotel Santa Fé and Cheyenne each of which has a western theme. The Sequoia Lodge and Newport Bay Club meanwhile both have the advantage of having indoor swimming pools (*closed on selected dates – please ask for details*). Whichever hotel you choose, you can be sure of a great Disneyland Paris quest experience!

The descriptions of hotels on pages 82 and 83 are from a brochure advertising coach holidays to Disneyland Paris.

Reading and Writing

Read the descriptions of the hotels, then write down the answers to these questions.

1 Which of the hotels is built as if it is part of a Hollywood Cowboy town?

2 Which hotel is built like a Mexican village?

3 Which hotel is surrounded by trees?

4 In which two hotels are there swimming pools?

5 In which hotel would you find these restaurants:
a The Cape Cod; **b** La Cantina; **c** Hunter's Grill; **d** Chuckwagon Cafe?

6 Which hotel has bunk beds in the bedrooms?

7 In which hotel are the bedrooms decorated in blue and white?

8 Which hotel has log fires in the main building in winter?

9 Which hotel plays country music in one of its bars?

10 Which hotel has a fiesta-style bar with live entertainment?

11 In which hotels are the shops called **a** the Northwest Passage boutique; **b** Bay Boutique?

12 Which of the hotels is the furthest away from the theme park?

In Groups

On your own, decide which hotel you would choose to stay in if you were going to Disneyland Paris. Then tell the other members of the group which hotel you chose and why.

Writing and Drawing

In pairs, plan a 30-second TV advertisement for one of the four hotels. Prepare a storyboard, giving full details of the series of pictures you would show and of the script for your advertisement.

A cosy mountain retreat set among lush trees, the **Sequoia Lodge** follows the traditions of the Great National Parks with a main lodge featuring a crackling fireplace in winter.

The hotel is only a ten minute stroll from the Theme Park, has its own health club and an indoor river rock themed swimming pool. Each themed bedroom has either one king-size or two double beds, plus bathroom.

You'll also enjoy the themed restaurants. Hunter's Grill has a rustic ambiance and serves spit-roasted meats and poultry, and Beaver Creek Tavern provides casual, family dining with generous salads and hamburgers etc. The Redwood Bar, a games room, children's playground and Northwest Passage boutique complete the facilities of this charming hotel.

A New England 'seaside resort' from the turn of the century featuring lakeside promenades and a delightful yacht club ambiance best describes the **Newport Bay Club**. Just a 10 minute lakeside stroll from the Theme Park the hotel boasts a superb, heated indoor pool with snack bar; a fully equipped health club with gym, massage facilities, sauna, steam room and solarium; a children's playground and games arcade.

Each crisp blue and white bedroom features one king-size or two double beds, plus bathroom. You can eat in style at the hotel's two restaurants. The Cape Cod serves Mediterranean-style seafood, pizza and pasta in a casual garden setting and the Yacht Club offers a speciality steak and seafood menu including whole Maine lobster. At the end of the day you can relax with a drink in Fisherman's Wharf old world lounge and a souvenir of your visit may be purchased from Bay Boutique.

The Hotel Santa Fe, a re-creation of a New Mexico Pueblo village, nestles on the banks of the Rio Grande, a 15 minute stroll from Disney Village and the Theme Park. The hotel features colourful landscaping, playful southwest decor and the Pueblo-themed rooms contain two double beds, plus bathroom.

The hotel's restaurant offers tasty food. La Cantina features typical Tex Mex specialities and the Rio Grande Bar offers live entertainment in a fiesta-style bar. There is also a Mexican ruin themed children's playground, a games arcade and the Trading Post for New Mexican giftware and Disney souvenirs.

More than a hotel, the **Hotel Cheyenne** is a Hollywood Cowboy town straight from the untamed frontiers. Just a 10 minute stroll from Disney Village and the Theme Park, the Hotel Cheyenne is a fun place to stay.

The 'Western'-style bedrooms feature one double bed and one set of bunk beds, plus a fully fitted bathroom. The Texan style Chuckwagon Cafe features a buffet of barbecue specialities and you can also enjoy country music and a drink in the Red Garter Saloon Bar.

Selling Your City

How would you describe your city, town or village, if you were advertising it in a holiday brochure to try to attract visitors?

Here's the description that Pippa wrote about her home town.

Basingstoke – The Best Break in Britain

Take a break in Basingstoke – see 'Doughnut City' for yourself. Yes, we have more roundabouts than any other town!

We can also boast an ultra-modern ice skating rink, a cinema complex, where you can watch the latest releases, and a ten-pin bowling alley.

Basingstoke is within easy reach of the New Forest, London, Portsmouth and the south coast. The nearby Hampshire countryside has more signed walks than anywhere else in Britain.

Whatever you want to do, whether it's to get away from it all and relax, or have a fun-filled family holiday, Basingstoke is the place to be.

Book your holiday in Basingstoke for the best break in Britain.

Speaking and Listening

1 Write an advertisement for a holiday brochure designed to attract visitors to your town or village. Think carefully about these questions before you write your first draft.

- What features do you want to include in your description?

- In what order are you going to put the information, so as to make your advertisement most effective?

- Can you think of a slogan that you can use, like Pippa's slogan 'Basingstoke for the best break in Britain'? (A **slogan** is a phrase used by advertisers to persuade you to do things or to buy things. See *English Direct 2*, pages 32–39.)

- What methods can you use to make your place sound attractive? (Look back over pages 80–83.)

When you have done the first draft of your advertisement, discuss it with a friend, then redraft it. Remember to check the spelling, punctuation and grammar. Finally, produce a neat copy of it on the word processor.

2 Now try writing a description designed to put people off visiting a particular place, rather than to attract them to it. Either make up your own name for it or call it Sludge-on-Sea.

Conjunctions

Remember that a **conjunction** is a joining word. Some common conjunctions are:

and, but, or, nor
after, as, before, since, until
when, whenever, while
where, wherever
how, however
as, because, since
although, if, unless.

A conjunction can be used to join two short sentences together to make one longer sentence. For example, instead of these two short sentences:

There were lots of things to do.
We had a good holiday.

you could write:

There were lots of things to do, <u>so</u> we had a good holiday.

or:

<u>*Because*</u> *there were lots of things to do, we had a good holiday.*

Exercise A

Join the two sentences to make one longer one by using a conjunction.

1 The sun is very strong. You should not lie in it for too long.
2 You will make lots of new friends. The people are very friendly.
3 You can go for long walks along the beach. You can go windsurfing in the bay.
4 You can hire a powerboat for the day. It will cost you a lot of money.
5 You stand on the clifftop to watch the sunset. You will have a spectacular view.
6 You will need to take a thick sweater. It sometimes gets cold at night.

Exercise B

Copy out these sentences, using conjunctions to fill in the gaps.

1 We ran into the sea, ... the water was colder than we expected ... we started to shiver.
2 There are lots of shops ... you can buy things very cheaply ... you are prepared to bargain.
3 ... it rained a lot, we had a good time ... there were plenty of places to visit.
4 ... you have visited the castle, you can go for a swim ... take a stroll through the market.
5 ... you go on the island, you will see people walking ... there are no motor vehicles.
6 ... you want a cheap holiday, you can go camping ... you can stay in a youth hostel.

Holiday Islands

Here are two descriptions of the island of Malta. The first is taken from a travel brochure; the second is from an encyclopedia.

Malta

Malta

An island of pale, honey-coloured rock emerges dramatically out of the blue-green Mediterranean between Sicily and North Africa. Malta may be just a tiny country – only seventeen miles by nine – but it is full of character. The rocky coves are a paradise for scuba-diving, sailing or fishing, and the beach at Mellieha Bay is clean and gently shelving.

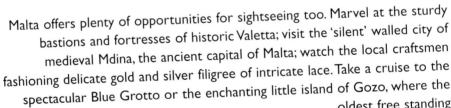

Malta offers plenty of opportunities for sightseeing too. Marvel at the sturdy bastions and fortresses of historic Valetta; visit the 'silent' walled city of medieval Mdina, the ancient capital of Malta; watch the local craftsmen fashioning delicate gold and silver filigree of intricate lace. Take a cruise to the spectacular Blue Grotto or the enchanting little island of Gozo, where the oldest free standing temples in the world are situated. In the evening, stop at one of the many friendly and reasonably priced restaurants to enjoy the good food and fine local wines.

MALTA is an island in the middle of the Mediterranean Sea, about 96 kilometres (60 miles) south of Sicily. Together with the other Maltese islands of Gozo and Comino it forms a small republic. The north and east coasts have a number of bays and natural harbours. There are hills in the south-west but they are not high. Malta has a pleasant warm climate but little rain falls and there are no rivers and few trees.

The Maltese are a people of mixed origin, but mostly Italian. Nearly all are Roman Catholic, and many have large families and are devoted to their children. The Maltese language is Arabic in origin but it has many Sicilian words. Many of the people speak English as well as Maltese.

The capital of Malta is Valetta, built on a steep peninsula which divides in two the magnificent Grand Harbour. Near by is the modern deep-water port of Marsamxett. On the south-east side of the harbour the three crowded cities of Vitoriosa, Cospicua and Senglea are clustered round the dockyard. The old capital of Notabile (in Maltese, Mdina) in the south-west hills contains the Cathedral Church of Malta and some picturesque early 15th-century palaces. The chief town in Gozo, which is a hillier and greener island than Malta, is Victoria (in Maltese, Rabat). Malta has some very interesting tombs and temples built of huge stone blocks at Hal Tarxien and elsewhere, from about 4000 BC.

Speaking and Listening

In pairs, read the two descriptions of Malta. Then discuss these questions.

● The aim of the writer of the travel brochure is to present selected facts about the island, so that you will want to visit it. Discuss how he or she tries:

a to make the island seem attractive in the first two sentences;

b to make the island appeal to people who like a beach holiday;

c to suggest that there is plenty to do for people who like to go sight-seeing.

● The aim of the writer of the encyclopedia article is to give you general information about the island. Discuss what you are told:

a about its position, landscape and climate (paragraph 1);

b about the people, their language and religion (paragraph 2);

c about the capital city and Malta's history (paragraph 3).

● Now that you have looked at the different types of information that the extracts include, talk about the different styles in which they are written. Notice how the second writer gives the facts in straightforward statements, using very few adjectives and writing in a formal way.

Discuss how the first writer writes in a more informal style, addressing the reader directly by inviting you to 'marvel at' the buildings and to 'take a cruise'. Pick out the words and phrases that are used to make Malta and what it has to offer seem attractive.

In this unit you will be expressing your opinions about soap operas and writing and filming your own soap.

Soap Operas

A **soap opera** is a popular television drama serial about people's daily lives. Here are some people saying what they think about soaps.

'I like the way British soaps tackle problems people really face – such as drug addiction, bullying, alcoholism and family quarrels.' – Hussain

'A good soap has characters in it that you can relate to.' – Lin

'Soaps mustn't be too realistic. Lots of ordinary life is routine and boring. Soaps have to focus on the dramatic moments.' – Sita

'The best episodes are the ones with cliffhanger endings.' – Frank

'Most soaps aren't multi-cultural enough.' – Tai

'The characters must be realistic. In many soaps all the adult characters are old-fashioned. The women are strong-minded working-class types and the men spend all their time down the pub, drinking and wheeling and dealing.' – Jasreen

'There need to be lots of different story-lines going on at the same time.' – Tracy

Speaking and Listening

- In groups, discuss each of the statements in turn and say why you agree or disagree with them
- Explain which is your favourite soap and why.
- Discuss what you think makes a good soap. Draw up a list of the features of a good soap. Then appoint someone to act as a spokesperson for the group and share your ideas in a class discussion.

Writing

- Write a review of your favourite soap.
- Imagine you are the director of your favourite soap and that you plan to introduce a new character into the series. Explain who the character is and how he or she will fit into the series.

How a soap is made

Writing the script

The script for a soap opera, such as *Eastenders* or *Coronation Street*, is developed by a team of people. The team consists of three groups – *producers, script editors* and *writers*.

The first stage is for the writers to produce **story outlines**. The story outlines consist of ideas for stories that develop over a number of episodes.

Then the team holds a series of meetings. At the first meeting, called a script conference, they discuss the story outlines. Next, there is a planning meeting at which the general outline for twelve episodes is decided. Finally, there is a meeting called a commissioning meeting. The general outline is discussed and the writers make sure they know what each episode is to be about.

The writers now have about four weeks in which to write the first draft of their script. The producer and script editor(s) then read and comment on the script. Often, they suggest changes and the writer has to redraft it. When the final copy of the script is ready, the production stage begins.

Producing an episode

The production team includes a *director, production manager, production assistant* and an *assistant floor manager*. They discuss how the script will be filmed and talk to the cast about it.

Each episode is rehearsed and recorded over a two-week period. During the first week, there are external recordings. In *Eastenders*, this is done in Albert Square. In the second week, three further days are needed for rehearsing and recording.

The productions are recorded and edited on videotape. After visual editing, the sound is recorded and mixed with appropriate background noise, such as traffic sounds, radios and door chimes.

Speaking and Listening

- In groups, read the article 'How a Soap is Made'. Discuss what you learn from it about **a** how a script is developed; **b** how an episode is produced.

- Choose a soap opera and work together to develop some suggestions for storylines for future episodes. Make notes of your ideas and appoint someone to act as a spokesperson. Then form a larger group with one of the other groups that chose to develop ideas for the same soap as your group. Role-play a story conference at which you discuss the different story ideas and choose the ones that you think are the best.

Creating Your Own Soap

Farhan and Stuart were asked by their teacher to develop ideas for a soap opera that had lots of teenage characters. Their teacher pointed out that they would need to think about three things – the characters, the setting and the storylines. After a lot of discussion, they decided to set their soap in an imaginary street in Leicester called Willoughby Street, and to call it 'Willoughby Youth', after the youth club in which a lot of the action was going to take place.

The Characters

Farhan and Stuart decided to have six main characters. Here are their notes on the characters.

Mr John Hyland (early forties). The youth club manager. A lonely divorcee. Determined to make a success of the club. Speaks with a lisp. Appears weak, but is stubborn.

Mrs Erma Patel (early fifties). A businesswoman who owns a chain of curry houses. Wants to use some of her wealth to help the community. Has strong ideas, but is too busy to put her ideas into practice.

Shaleem Mundar (aged 16). Friend of Charmaine. More level-headed. Wants to get GCSEs and go to college. The person who cares.

Charmaine Beechwood (aged 16). School truant. Smokes and drinks. Lives with Mum and much younger sister. Parents divorced.

Sunil Thakrar (aged 18). Goes to college. Enthusiastic but rather shy.

Leonard Charles (aged 18). Parents moved to Leicester from West London. Wants to be in a pop group one day. Has a quick wit and fancies himself as a 'rap' poet.

The Setting

Any soap opera needs a number of different sets (acting areas). Farhan and Stuart's teacher had pointed out that most soap operas need an area like a row of houses, a pub or coffee bar, which can act as a meeting-place for the characters. That's one of the reasons why Farhan and Stuart chose to develop their series around a youth centre.

They decided their soap would have five main sets. Here are their notes on the sets.

Willoughby Youth Club – a big hall, a smaller office/meeting room and the area outside the main entrance.

The Patel house – lounge, kitchen and bedrooms.

Mr Hyland's house – a lounge and kitchen/dining-room.

Stert Street School – the playground, dining-hall and one classroom.

One of Mrs Patel's curry houses – the kitchen and restaurant.

Storyline

Here is Farhan and Stuart's storyline for Episode 1.

Episode 1

Charmaine tells three characters – Jake, Damian and Molly – about some cash she saw Mr Hyland putting in the safe at Willoughby Youth Centre. The three decide to break in and steal the cash, which is Mrs Patel's donation for a summer outing.

Mr Hyland has already warned the group that there's been too much trouble recently – if there are any more break-ins or vandalism the club will close.

Charmaine feels guilty. She doesn't want to get the blame for the club closing. She tells Shaleem what she's done. They can't find Mr Hyland, so they decide to go to the curry house to tell Mrs Patel.

Mrs Patel isn't there. Her daughter has been rushed to hospital with a suspected broken arm. Charmaine and Shaleem discuss going to the police, but Charmaine doesn't want to. They go and hide outside the youth club to wait for the thieves.

Speaking and Listening

In groups, discuss Farhan and Stuart's ideas.

- What do you think of **a** their characters; **b** their setting; **c** their first storyline?
- Say whether you think their ideas would work and discuss any changes you would make. Would you change any of the characters, add any new characters or leave any of them out? Would you change any of their settings?

In Pairs

Study the other storylines for 'Willoughby Youth' (right) that Farhan and Stuart's class suggested. Which ones do you think would work? Discuss why and make a list of those you think are the most interesting and worth developing. Then join up with another pair and share your ideas. Together work out some other possible storylines for 'Willoughby Youth' and present them to the rest of the class.

Writing

Work with a partner. Develop your own ideas for a soap opera in which many of the characters are teenagers. Write out details of the characters, the setting and the storyline for the first episode, in the way that Farhan and Stuart did.

Storylines for Willoughby Youth

1 Charmaine and Shaleem fall out. Shaleem is spending all her time studying. Charmaine threatens to end their friendship if Shaleem won't go to London with her on a shopping spree.

2 Leonard Charles is beaten up in a racial attack. Although the regular club members rally round, Leonard says he's leaving. But not before he's had an audition to join a pop group called The Flip Raps.

3 Mr Patel is opening the youth club's new snack bar when he suffers a heart-attack. As he lies in intensive care, everyone worries about the future of the club. Without his cash support, it may have to close.

4 The youth club members hold a series of fund-raising events for a local charity. There is an article about them in the local newspaper and they appear on TV.

Writing a TV Script

The Setting

When you are writing a TV script, you have to think not only about what the characters are saying, but about what pictures you want to be seen on the screen.

Here is part of a TV script by Anthony Horowitz from an episode of the series *Starting Out*. The two characters in these scenes are unemployed teenagers – Mike Williams, a white boy, and Leo Young, a black boy.

Use the key on page 93 to understand the technical terms.

SCENE NINE

Int. Fast food restaurant 2.00 p.m.

> *Mike* AND *Leo* ARE EATING PIZZAS IN A FAST FOOD RESTAURANT. THEY ARE CLOSE TO THE DOOR. THEIR MEAL IS ALMOST OVER.

Mike   What would you do for money?

Leo   What wouldn't I do?

Mike   No. I'm talking about easy money.

Leo   No such thing.

Mike   Listen. I was down the pub last week, right? The Four Feathers. And this old bird came in. Had a half of Guinness and then left. Are you with me?

Leo   What? She bought you a Guinness, too?

Mike   No. It's just, some of the punters were talking about her ...

> CUT TO:

SCENE TEN

Ext. Maggie Lambert's house 2.00 p.m.

> *Maggie Lambert* WALKS HOME, CARRYING HER SHOPPING. SHE GOES INTO THE FRONT DOOR.

Mike   [V/O] Apparently, she's really stacked. She's got hundreds of pounds.

Leo   [V/O] In the bank?

Mike   [V/O] No. That's just the thing.

> CUT TO:

SCENE ELEVEN

Int. Maggie's bedroom 2.15 p.m.

> *Maggie* GOES INTO A SMALL, COMFORTABLE AND WELL-DECORATED BEDROOM. SHE APPROACHES THE BED.

Mike   [V/O] You know what old people are like. Keeps it under the mattress, doesn't she?

> *Maggie* TURNS THE MATTRESS UP. THERE ARE HUNDREDS OF POUNDS UNDERNEATH IT, ALL CRISP NEW FIVERS. SHE TAKES OUT A WAD AND BEGINS TO COUNT IT.

Mike   [V/O] Likes to count it last thing before she goes to bed.

> CUT TO:

SCENE TWELVE

Int. Fast food restaurant 2.20 p.m.

AS BEFORE

Leo	You're kidding me.
Mike	That's what they said.
Leo	No. I mean – you wouldn't ...
Mike	Why not?
Leo	An old lady!
Mike	She doesn't need it.
Leo	Do you?
Mike	I'm skint.
Leo	Then how are you going to pay for this?
Mike	You finished?
Leo	Yeah.

Mike LOOKS ROUND THE RESTAURANT. THERE ARE NO WAITERS OR WAITRESSES NEAR THEM.

Mike   Now!

Mike GETS UP AND MOVES QUICKLY OUT OF THE FRONT DOOR – WITHOUT PAYING.

Leo   Mike!

Leo HAS NO CHOICE THIS TIME. HE GETS UP AND FOLLOWS.

CUT TO: ANOTHER ANGLE. THE *Manager* SEES THEM GO.

Manager   Oy!

THE *Manager* SPRINTS FOR THE DOOR.

Key

Int. means 'interior' and indicates that the scene takes place indoors.

Ext. means 'exterior' and indicates that the scene takes place outdoors.

V/O means 'voice over' and shows that someone who cannot be seen on the screen is speaking.

CUT TO indicates that the picture changes. The picture on the screen is cut off and replaced by one from another angle or of another scene.

Writing

Work in pairs, and together draft the script for the first episode of your own soap opera. Before you begin, study the layout of Anthony Horowitz's script. Then follow these instructions to make sure you lay your script out properly.

- Start with details of where the scene takes place and indicate whether it is indoors or outdoors.

- In capital letters, state what the characters are seen doing at the start of the scene.

- Put the name of the person speaking in the margin.

- Every time a new person speaks, start a new line.

- Do not use speech marks.

- Use capital letters to give details of any important moves the characters have to make or to indicate any change of picture or camera angle.

Reading and Writing

In pairs, read the script. Then, on your own, write answers to these questions.

1 Where and when does scene nine take place?

2 Which pub does Mike tell Leo he was in and who does he say he saw there?

3 What is shown on the screen during scene ten?

4 Where and when does scene eleven take place?

5 In scene twelve how does Leo react to what Mike has told him in scenes ten and eleven?

6 Explain exactly what happens at the end of scene twelve.

Register

The way you speak varies according to the situation. When you are with your friends in an informal situation, you will speak in a chatty, conversational style. When you are in a more formal situation, for example being interviewed for a job or making a complaint in a shop, you will use more formal language. A style of speaking or writing which is used in a particular situation is called a **register**.

On the right, Darren is talking to two different people about the same incident and using two different registers. When talking to his friend (Extract A) he uses an *informal* register. When talking to a teacher (Extract B) he uses a more *formal* register.

Extract A

We were playing footie. Biggsy gave the ball a right whack. It smacked against the tree and whizzed straight through the window of Jacko's classroom. We all scarpered, 'cause we knew Jacko'd do his nut.

Extract B

We were playing football and Biggs kicked the ball so hard that it bounced off the tree. It went straight through Mr Jackson's window. We knew he'd be very angry, so we ran off.

In Pairs

1 How is Darren's language different in the two extracts? Which features of the language show that in Extract A he is talking informally and in Extract B he is talking formally?

2 Choose two situations from the list below – one in which the speakers are using language informally, and the other in which the speakers are using language formally. Then role-play the scenes for the rest of the class and discuss how you tried to show the differences in register.

- Two schoolchildren gossiping about a friend.
- A student showing a visitor round the school.
- A customer returning a faulty item and asking for a refund.
- An argument between two children about whose turn it is to do the washing-up.
- A television reporter talking to a student who has raised money for charity by taking part in a sponsored event.
- Two people talking about how they spent a day at the seaside.

Slang

Slang is the term used to describe very informal words and expressions. Since most writing is formal, slang words and expressions are inappropriate in most pieces of writing. However, speech is often full of slang.

Here are some examples of slang. The slang word or expression has been underlined and its meaning is given in the brackets.

I'll be back in a jiffy (very quickly).

You shut your trap (mouth).

Those trainers are dead cool (very smart and fashionable).

Exercise A

Copy out these sentences. Underline the slang words and expressions and put their meanings in brackets. If necessary, use a dictionary to help you.

1 The copper started to chase us, so we legged it.

2 There was no grub left, because they'd scoffed the lot.

3 There were two geezers sitting in an old banger.

4 The centre forward missed a sitter, so the crowd gave him stick.

5 Sam was cheesed off, because someone had nicked her pencil case.

6 My Mum rabbited on at me when she found out I'd been skiving.

7 He told us to belt up and clear off.

8 Dad flipped his lid when Mum chucked out his best suit by mistake.

9 The place was really grotty but the band was groovy.

10 We splashed out a lot of money, but they ripped us off.

Exercise B

In the speech below, Tracy has used a lot of slang expressions, which would be inappropriate in a piece of writing. Copy it out, replacing the slang expressions with ones that would be more suitable in a piece of writing.

Greg Cranston is a right twit. He thinks he's being smart but he's a real pain. He's always being lippy to the teachers. He got what was coming to him when Mr Jones had a go at him. He needs to learn to shut his gob or he'll land himself in it good and proper.

Glossary and Index

Adjective An adjective is a word that tells you more about a noun, for example 'delicious' or 'red'. *See pages 13 and 80.*

Adverb An adverb is a word that tells you more about a verb, for example 'brightly' or 'quickly'. *See page 13.*

Alliteration Alliteration is the use of several words together that all begin with the same sound. *See page 80.*

Ballad A ballad is a type of poem that tells a story. It usually consists of a number of short verses with a strong beat or rhythm to keep the story moving at a fast pace. *See pages 40–45.*

Comedy A comedy is a play that tells a light-hearted story with a happy ending. *See page 60.*

Comma A comma is a punctuation mark used to break up lists of words and to separate the different parts of long sentences. *See page 30.*

Conjunction A conjunction is a word that joins words or sentences. *See page 85.*

Debate A debate is a formal discussion in which opposing views are expressed. *See pages 38–39.*

DTP DTP is an abbreviation for 'desk-top publishing'. A DTP program can be used to design and produce newspapers and other material on a computer. *See pages 78–79.*

Editorial An editorial is an article in a newspaper that expresses an opinion on a particular topic in the news. *See page 75.*

Epitaph An epitaph is a short piece of writing that is put on the gravestone of a person who has died. *See page 68.*

Feature article A feature article is an article in a newspaper or magazine that covers a topic in an extensive and interesting way. *See pages 76–77.*

First-person narrative Telling a story from the viewpoint of one of the characters is called first-person narrative. *See page 58.*

Homophone A homophone is a word that sounds the same as another word, but has a different meaning and a different spelling. *See page 31.*

Motion A motion is a proposal that people speak for or against at a debate. *See pages 38–39.*

Obituary An obituary is a piece of writing about the life and achievements of someone who has just died. *See page 68.*

Paragraph A paragraph is a group of sentences, all of which are about the same idea or subject. *See page 17.*

Pen portrait A pen portrait is a paragraph that tells you some key information about a character. *See page 50.*

Prefix A prefix is a group of letters that is added in front of a word to make a new word. *See page 12.*

Questionnaire A questionnaire is a list of questions which can be used to find out people's views. *See page 71.*

Rap A rap, or rap poem, has a strong rhythmic beat and is often spoken to music. Raps are written to be spoken and performed. *See pages 46–49.*

Register A register is a style of speaking or writing which is used in a particular situation. It may be formal or informal. *See page 94.*

Rhetorical question A rhetorical question is one that does not require an answer. Such questions can be used for dramatic effect in an argument or speech. *See page 33.*

Sentence A sentence is something written or spoken that makes sense. It always begins with a capital letter, and must end with either a full stop, a question mark or an exclamation mark. *See page 17.*

Slang Slang is the term used to describe very informal words and expressions. Speech is often full of slang. *See page 95.*

Slogan A slogan is a phrase used by advertisers to persuade you to do things or to buy things. *See page 84.*

Soap opera A soap opera is a popular television drama serial about people's daily lives. *See pages 88–93.*

Story outline A story outline is a writer's ideas for stories that develop over a number of episodes of a soap opera or serial. *See page 89.*

Subject The subject of a sentence is the person or thing doing the action described by the main verb in the sentence. *See page 30.*

Suffix A suffix is a group of letters that is added to the end of a word to make a new word. *See page 13.*

Third-person narrative Telling a story from the outside, as if you are someone who knows all about the events and the people involved, is called third-person narrative. *See page 58.*

Tragedy A tragedy is a play that tells a sad story, often ending in the death of the main character. *See page 60.*